AFRO-CUBAN RELIGIONS

Markus Wiener Publishers
Princeton

Ian Randle Publishers
Kingston

AFRO-CUBAN RELIGIONS

Miguel Barnet

Translated from Spanish by
Christine Renata Ayorinde

For information write to:
Markus Wiener Publishers
231 Nassau Street, Princeton, NJ 08542
www.markuswiener.com

Library of Congress Cataloging-in-Publication Data

Barnet, Miguel, 1940–
    [Cultos afrocubanos. English]
    Afro-Cuban Religions/Miguel Barnet; translated from Spanish
        by Christine Ayorinde.
    Includes bibliographical references.
    ISBN-13: 978-1-55876-254-1 (hardcover)
    ISBN-10: 1-55876-254-X (hardcover)
    ISBN-13: 978-1-55876-255-8 (paperback)
    ISBN-10: 1-55876-255-8 (paperback)
    1. Blacks—Cuba—Religion.   2. Cuba—Religion.   I. Title.
    BL2530.C9B3713 2001
    299'.6'097291—dc21

                                                    00-054638

First published in Jamaica 2001 by
Ian Randle Publishers
11 Cunningham Avenue, Kingston 6, Jamaica
ISBN 976-637-054-0 paperback
A catalogue record for this book is available from the
National Library of Jamaica.

Printed in the United States of America on acid-free paper.

CONTENTS

FOREWORD

Any nation that betrays its principles is close to suicide. As an Afro-Cuban proverb says: The billy-goat that tramples on a drum must pay with its hide.

—*Fernando Ortiz*

"Would the reader like to taste the waters of the African fount that established itself on Cuban soil?" inquires Alfonso Reyes in his introduction to Fernando Ortiz's work, *Los bailes y el teatro de los negros en el folklore de Cuba* (The Dances and Theater of Blacks in Cuban Folklore). To that end he recommends reading the works of the master of Cuban ethnology. The mysterious fount referred to by Reyes is full of ancient mysteries and invites the reader to immerse himself. Before doing so he must first obtain a compass. This book is simply intended to provide the reader with the compass to show him the way. Exploring the fantasy-rich world of legends with its manifold and overlapping contradictory versions is a unique and unforgettable experience. However, it can also lead to confusion when the reasons behind the migration and syncretism of certain themes are not apparent to the reader.

These chapters are intended to thin out the dense undergrowth of the Cuban forest. They deal with traits of Yoruba and Bantu origin. These are not only still in existence today but in fact are flourishing magnificently. They are organized in such a way that they are readily accessible even to readers with little prior knowledge of the subject.

A great deal has been written about what is termed Santería or Regla de Ocha and about the religions of the Congos[1] or the Regla de Palo Monte. Yet specialists have tended to focus on liturgy and theology rather than on the more general issues and the origins of these religions. Once the family ties of the Africans brought to Cuba disintegrated, the cults were forced to restructure themselves, and they became acclimatized to Cuban conditions, as Alfonso Reyes has rightly pointed out. This gave rise to a peculiar process of transculturation whereby certain elements asserted themselves over others. Tutelary deities receded into the background, while other deities that had not been especially important in their places of origin stepped into the foreground and assumed an elevated position in the hierarchy. In this way a system of cults developed that has its origin in Africa—Nigeria or the lands of the Congo River—but which may be described as independent national creations.

The Regla de Ocha or Santería and the Regla de Palo Monte are the result of the process of transculturation of elements that took root in Cuba. These elements have provided us with a powerful zest that gives Cuban culture its unique flavor.

—*Miguel Barnet*

The Role of the Myth in Cuban Culture

Image of Osun

T he myth in Cuban culture, strictly speaking, refers to the myths of African origin that were brought by the slaves. These myths were preserved in the religions of the various ethnic groups who populated the island during the period of the slave trade. Their breeding ground was the sugar mill, which became the focal point of the society that emerged under the plantation system.

All mythological systems tend to describe the origins and exploits of a group of interrelated gods—a pantheon. This is especially true of Afro-Cuban myths. They tell of the deities' adventures, everyday pursuits, festivities, fraternal and sexual relationships, conflicts and other matters. Their purpose is to explain the rituals in which these events appear and also the religion and society. These myths—now transculturated[2]—have been preserved in almost all the religions of African origin that are practiced throughout the country. They are found in the Abakuá society, and in the practices of the Arará and of the Yoruba,[3] where the myths are known as *pwataki*.[4] They have a universal appeal. The myths have spread throughout the island as simple tales told by the common people in a natural manner that is remarkable for the way it deals with ordinary, nonreligious themes. Thus the more esoteric myths are gradually disappear-

Canastillero (cabinet in which religious attributes of the orishas are kept)
Top shelf: soperas (bowls used as containers for religious objects) of Obatalá;
middle shelf: soperas of Ochún; bottom shelf: soperas of Yemayá

ing, incorporating secular material and becoming folktales. Little by little, they are losing their religious essence and turning into popular tales that are almost functional, while still retaining their original qualities and beauty. They are functional because, although the myths have a religious purpose, ordinary people use them to explain many things. Characters such as Changó, the god of fire and lightning, or Ochún, the goddess of love and gold, are identified with real people in society and act as the models for various personality types.

On the other hand, there are the legends dealing with subjects such as death or work and also mythological fables and tales about the gods. Most of these are of Yoruba origin, and they are highly representative of the Cuban oral tradition. They contain interesting examples of cultural change such as when a god is given the title of Secretary of the Supreme Court or Fire Chief.

A study of the mythology can give us an insight into the mind-set of those Cubans who practice the religions. The myths are also an indispensable complement to the divination systems and are thus important for deciphering their mysteries. In fact, all the divination systems used in the Afro-Cuban religions have a rich mythological base. For example, each *letra* or sign produced by throwing the coconut shells or traced on the Ifa divining tray (Ifá is the god of divination) has one or more related pwatakí. These tell the client why he should perform a particular magical work or choose a course of action. In most cases, the protagonists of the stories are the gods themselves. Thus the example of Elegguá, Olofi or Yemayá can suggest particular models of behavior or an immediate physical or spiritual course of action.

Other stories admonish, advise or warn the client. For instance: "Ifá says that the Virgin of Charity (Ochún) is annoyed with you, and if you do not yet have a child it is because she does

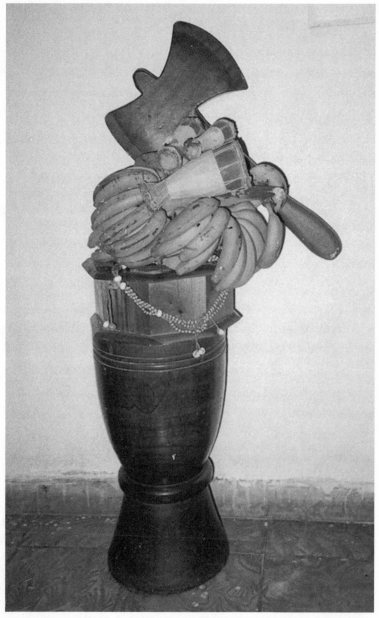

Batea (wooden bowl) de Chango on pilón (mortar) with offering of plantain.
He is the lord of the batá drums (on top).
The double ax symbolizes his aché (sacred power).

not wish it. However, you are meant to have one. You must pay that which you have promised and receive Orula so that those who did not respect him will be compelled to do so." Like this example, many pwataki govern aspects of human existence.

There are numerous examples in which forces of nature such as lightning or storms, or animals like the dog or tortoise, play an active part in the plot. "Changó hurled a thunderbolt at Oggún in his forge"; "A flash of lightning shattered the bars of the prison and Changó escaped"; "Babalú Ayé wanders through the bush with his dogs. He never leaves home without them"; "Osaín was born from the head of a tortoise."

Believers do not need to ponder the legitimacy of a myth. In their simple, direct and natural way they take it at face value. "Things are the way they are because that is the way they are"; "Changó was king because he was king." Like people describing an insignificant part of their daily routine and, without pausing for breath, they will recount the most unbelievable exploits, full of fantasy and surrealism. Don't they say that when it thunders it is because the saints are moving the furniture about in the sky? Or that it is the snorting of an enraged Changó? For a santero, sea currents, storms and shipwrecks are all the willful acts of Yemayá, the goddess of the sea. There are numerous examples of the rich imagination of the common people.

One striking thing about the logical processes through which these myths became acculturated is the way people mold them to suit changing conditions in society. Every African myth in circulation in Cuba has been adapted to fit its new environment. Elements necessary for integration into Cuban society and the western world are introduced, and the myths are noticeably influenced by the environment.

In Africa, Ochún washes her clothes on stones in a river, but in

Cuba she uses a washtub and even—why not?—an electric iron. Or take the case of Oggún, god of iron and war, who in Cuba is also the patron of mechanics, railway workers, truck drivers and anything related to metal, specifically iron. This is one of the most unusual and remarkable features of Afro-Cuban mythology. It demonstrates perfectly the force of the popular imagination and its capacity for substituting elements and even adapting philosophical values to suit new social situations.

Controversial themes such as incest are recounted in variant versions of the tales. Sometimes incest is treated as a normal occurrence, as when Changó has sexual relations with his mother, Yemayá. At other times it is prevented from taking place:

> The lord of the river, Aggayú, had a love affair with Yemayá. Aggayú and Yemayá gave birth to Changó, but Yemayá abandoned him, and it was Obatalá who took him in and raised him. Claiming him as her son, she placed a necklace of white and crimson beads around his neck. She said that he would be king of the world, and she built him a castle. So it was that Changó reached manhood not knowing that his real mother was Yemayá and that Aggayú was his father. Without realizing that she was his mother, he wished to take Yemayá as his wife. A slave who followed Changó everywhere warned Yemayá, and before committing the sin she said to him: "Omo mí."[5] "I have no mother," replied Changó. Yemayá then said to him "Lubbeo,"[6] and offered him her breast. Changó recognized his mother and burst into tears.

There is also the story, set in the land of Mina, of the love affair between mother and son. Here Yemayá once again avoids committing incest and instead teaches her son a lesson:

Alafi (Changó) arrived in Yemaya's native land and fell in love with her at a party without realizing that she was his mother. Yemayá told him that she loved him too and that he should visit her at home.

"That vast blue expanse you can see in the distance is my home," and she pointed at the sea.

"Do we have to go there? I don't know how to swim, but if you take me I will go." They walked toward the shore.

"We have to go in farther."

"I can't swim," repeated Changó.

Yemayá jumped into her boat, made Changó climb in and rowed out to sea. The coast disappeared from view. Yemayá dived into the water and descended to the bottom. As she sank, an enormous wave overturned the boat, and Changó fell into the water. He grabbed the side of the boat and struggled to save himself from drowning. Yemayá, returning to the surface, saw Changó desperately shouting and calling for help. But she didn't move and, laughing at him, made no attempt to help.

At that moment Obatalá appeared, borne on the back of a majá-snake. She said, "Adyaguá Orissaego" (Yemayá, do not let your son die).

Yemayá answered, "Alakkata Oni feba Orissa Neghwa." (I will save you but from now on you must respect your Iyá [mother]).

"Cofieddano, Iyá mi." (Thank you, mother. I did not know that you were my mother).

Yemayá righted the boat and helped Changó climb in. He then asked the two saints: "Which one of you brought me into the world?"

"Yemayá," answered the Merciful Virgin. "I looked after you, but she gave birth to you."

Changó and Yemayá embraced on the sea. Whenever there is a batá drum ceremony and both

*Homage to Yemayá, improvised house altar of an akpwon
(person who leads the ritual singing at the orisha ceremonies)
as found throughout Cuba*

these saints come down, Changó, who claims that,
after God, there is no one more saintly than he, hum-
bles himself before both his mothers. He respects both
of them, and they calm him down when he gets carried away.

These risqué themes are recited by old Cuban griots, often
with a degree of reserve. However, with a little patience and sen-
sitivity one may hear them recount a wide range of myths with
the most improbable variants, as well as those dealing with more
classic themes.

Of course, in order to be able to compare these myths with those from other cultures and to find similarities between them, one needs a thorough knowledge of stories and myths from all over the world. One should also be well versed in history and ethnology. Nevertheless, anyone with a keen eye may spot similarities and common themes such as the creation of the universe, death, the deification of kings and so forth.

In Cuba these themes abound, especially "in the deep well of the African religions," as Alfonso Reyes would say. They are contained in the myths, legends, folktales and tales of fantasy. These themes came from another continent with those who were taken across the ocean against their will. Here they have taken root, soaked up different sap and been transformed, helping to bring forth leaves on the tree of our culture.

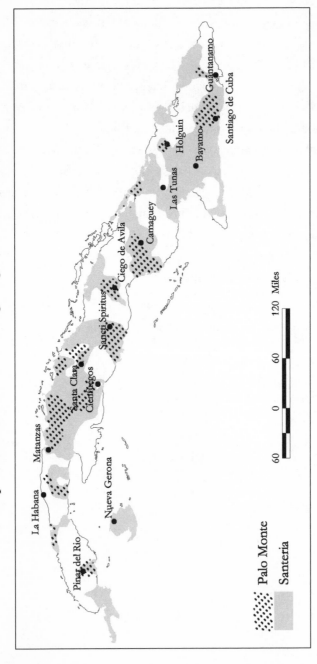

Principal manifestations of existing religions in today's Cuba.

Santeria and Palo Monte

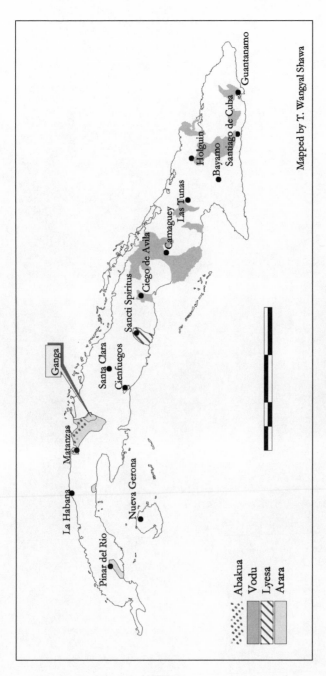

Other religious manifestations

Mapped by T. Wangyal Shawa

The Regla de Ocha

La Caridad del Cobre, patron saint of the island of Cuba,
identified with Ochún

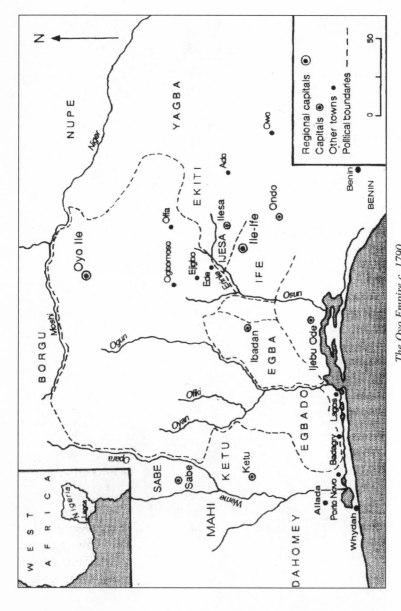

The Oyo Empire c. 1790.

From Robin Law, The Oyo Empire c. 1600–c. 1836: A West African imperialism in the era of the Atlantic Slave Trade *(Clarendon Press, 1977).*

F rom the mid-sixteenth century onward, large numbers of
slaves from Africa began to arrive in Cuba. They were
forced to work on the plantations producing coffee, other
minor crops and what later became the colony's greatest source
of wealth: sugar cane. The slaves, who came from many different regions of Africa bringing their cultures with them, were cas-
tigated first by their Spanish masters and then by the Creole
sugar barons. Brutally snatched from the coast of the Gulf of
Guinea and the forests of the deepest Congo, they became a profitable commodity in the most cruel and inhumane traffic that history has ever seen: the slave trade. Among the peoples from sub-
Saharan West Africa, those of Yoruba origin had the greatest
influence on the integrative processes of the island's cultural and
religious system. Within a short time they managed to dissemi-
nate their forms of expression. In the process they visibly influenced other African cultures, including those that had become
established in Cuba long before that of the Yoruba. For this reason, any attempt to portray the relationships between the deities,
rituals and liturgies of the respective African religious systems
must inevitably refer to the dominant models of Yoruba origin.

Elements of this culture, which has a richer and more complex
superstructure than the others, provided the framework for the

development and adaptation of the transculturated expressions that constitute Cuba's cultural heritage. Comparable in its richness and poetry to that of ancient Greece, Yoruba mythology offers the only consistent body of ideas about the creation of the world to be found among the treasures of Cuba's traditional popular culture. Yoruba mythology was transplanted in Cuba at various points in history and as part of a continuous and intensive process during the sugar boom of the late eighteenth and early nineteenth centuries, which led to an increase in slave imports. The mythology experienced fundamental changes as a result of the encounter, or sometimes clash, with other religions of African origin and with Roman Catholicism. This produced a spontaneous syncretism that engendered new cosmogonic values and the equation of Yoruba divinities with Roman Catholic saints.

The result of this syncretism was the religious complex known as Santería—a system of beliefs and rituals centered around the worship of the *orishas*[7] of the Nigerian Yoruba pantheon and their Catholic saint counterparts. This religion, perhaps as widely practiced in Cuba as the hybrid form known as popular spiritism, has as its basis the concept of a supreme trinity consisting of Olofi,[8] Oloddumare[9] and Olorun.[10] They have authority over the other orishas but are not themselves the objects of worship nor do they have a direct cult. The orishas are deemed to be their subjects and messengers on earth, and they are worshiped directly, have personal cults and are not considered abstract or noble entities. They intercede before Olofi on behalf of human beings through Obbatalá, the Supreme Judge or Principal Messenger, and can either reward or punish them depending on their everyday conduct.

Pierre Fatumbi Verger's book *Orixás* provides a useful explanation[11]:

Formerly the concept of *òrìsà* appeared relatively straightforward if one accepted the definitions offered in the work of a number of authors of the latter half of the last century and the early decades of this, who often copied indiscriminately from each other. However, a deeper analysis inclines us to maintain that it is in fact a more complex entity. Leo Frobenius was the first to point out, in 1910, that "the religion of the Yoruba became homogeneous by degrees only. Its present uniformity is the result of long evolution and the confluence of beliefs from different sources." Today, 70 years on, a single, organised and structured pantheon of the *orishas* is not to be found anywhere in the so-called "Yoruba" territory. The local variants show that *orishas* who occupy a dominant position in some areas are completely absent in others. The Shango cult, which predominates in Oyo, does not officially exist in Ife where a local deity, Oramfe, replaces him as the god of thunder. Oshun, whose cult is very important in the Ijesha region, is not found in the Egba region. Yemoja, the queen of the Egba region, is unknown in Ijesha. The position of all these *orishas* depends to large extent on the history of the cities of which they are tutelary deities. During his lifetime Shango was the third king of Oyo. In Oshogbo, Oshun made a pact with Laro, founder of the local royal dynasty. This is why water is always in abundant supply there. Odudua, founder of the city of Ife, whose sons became kings of other Yoruba city-states, had a persona which was more historical and political than divine. As we will see, those charged with invoking Odudua at ceremonies do not fall into possession trance and this underlines his temporal nature.

The standing of an *orisha* within the social structure will vary depending on whether the *orisha* represents a city with a royal palace (*àláfin*) inhabited by a

Canastillero containing religious attributes of the orishas

king (*alàdé*) who is entitled to wear a beaded crown (*adé*) which conceals his face, or whether he represents a city where the chief or Balè is only entitled to wear a more modest crown called an *àkòro*, and where the palace (*ilé Olójà*) is the home of the lord of the town market. In each case, the *orisha* serves to reinforce the power of the king or chief. The *orisha* is more or less at his disposal to guarantee and defend the stability and continuity of the dynasty and the protection of its subjects. However, in independent villages where civil power is weak, "in the absence of the (authoritarian) State the traditional religions have a much stronger influence and it is the 'fetish' priests who guarantee social cohesion."

The cults of certain *orishas* are found almost everywhere in Yorubaland. For example, the cult of the god of creation *Òrìsàálá*, also known as Obbatala, extends into the neighbouring territory of Dahomey, where he is known as Lisa. His wife *Yemowo* becomes *Mawu*, the "Supreme Deity" of the Fon. Ogun, the god of blacksmiths and ironworkers, has a function which makes him important outside his place of origin.

Sometimes a number of deities cover the same areas of responsibility in different regions: Shango in Oyo, Oramfe in Ife and Aira in Shabe are all lords of thunder. Ogun has warrior and hunter rivals in various places: Ija in Oyo and environs, *Òsóòsi* in Ketu, *Òre* in Ife and *Lògunède*, *Ibaùalámo* and *Erinlè* in the Ijesha region. *Òsanyìn* performs the same healing function among the Oyo as does *Elèsije* in Ife. *Aje Saluga* in Ife, and further to the west, *Òsùmàrè*, are both gods of wealth.

The case of *Nànà Buruku* or *Brukung* deserves separate consideration. This deity is the Supreme Goddess in western Yorubaland and also in more distant areas where the influence of Ife is less pronounced. In these places, although the cult of *Obbatalá* and *Òrìsàálá* is unknown, paradoxically, there are towns called Añá or Ife.

In the face of such extreme diversity and the multiple variations in the relationship between the *orishas*, overly structured representations do not prove convincing.

The orisha religion is linked to the idea of family. The extended family originates from a common ancestor and includes both the living and the dead. Once the system of tribal or family lineage fell apart, a religious brotherhood developed that united godparents (*padrinos*) and their godchildren (*ahijados*) in a series of close and inclusive horizontal relationships that extend beyond blood ties. One of the most distinctive features of Cuban Santería is the way in which a godfather (*padrino*) or godmother (*madrina*) becomes father or mother to numerous children who are members of a sort of cult group, popularly known as the *línea de santo* (line of the saint).

The orisha is essentially a deified ancestor who during his lifetime became linked with natural forces such as thunder, the wind and fresh or salt water. He is also skilled in certain activities such as hunting and metalwork as well as the properties and use of plants. After his death, the power or *aché* of the orisha-ancestor should have the capacity to be incarnated momentarily in one of his descendants during an instance of possession induced by the orisha.

When these exceptional beings who possess powerful aché pass from life on earth to the state of orisha, this occurs, as Verger has pointed out, in a moment of passion that is commemorated in legend. For example, Changó underwent such a transformation

Center: Antena de Egun (altar for ancestors) with typical offerigs:
glass of fresh water, glass of sugared water, bitter coffee,
cigarettes, cigars, flowers, fruits, candle.
Bottom left: clay bowl with Omiero (herbal brew used for ritual cleansing).
Top left: Siete Rayos (lit seven bolts of lightning;
Congo version of Changó or St. Barbara) with an offering of plantains.
Floor: ordus for Eggun (Ifá signs for the ancestors).

when, incensed because he had destroyed his palace and all his relatives, he climbed the hill at Igbeti near old Oyo to test the effectiveness of a preparation for causing lightning. In another legend, Changó transformed himself into an orisha or *ebora*[12] in a moment of vexation when he felt lonely after leaving Oyo to return to the region of Tapá. His first wife, Oyá, accompanied him into exile, and later, when Changó disappeared, she sank into the earth. His two other wives, Ochún and Oba, fearfully fleeing

the blazing wrath of their common husband, turned themselves
into the rivers that bear their names. Oggún was transformed into
an orisha when, lamenting bitterly, he realized that in a moment
of unthinking rage he had massacred the inhabitants of Ire, the
city he had founded. On his return, years later, no one recognized
him.

These deified ancestors did not die natural deaths of the sort
the Yoruba describe as the spirit departing the body. As they possessed very powerful aché and exceptional powers, they underwent a metamorphosis in moments of emotional crisis brought on
by anger or other strong sentiments. The material part of them
disappeared, consumed by this passion, leaving only the aché—
power in the form of pure energy.

As Verger explains in his *Orixás*,

> . . . is a pure form, immaterial *àse* which is only per-
> ceived by humans when it is embodied in one of them.
> The person chosen by the *orisha*, one of his descen-
> dants, is called *elégùn*——someone who is privileged
> to be "mounted" (*gún*) by him. This person becomes
> the vehicle which enables the *orisha* to return to earth
> to visit the descendants who invoke him and to receive
> tokens of respect from them.
>
> [. . .] *Orisha*, deified ancestor, is inherited within a
> family and passed down through the paternal line. The
> heads of extended families, the *balè*, usually delegate
> responsibility for the family *orisha* cult to an *aláàse*,
> the guardian of the god's power. They tend the cult
> with the help of the *elégùn*, who become possessed by
> the *orisha* under certain circumstances.
>
> The women of the family take part in the cere-
> monies and can become *elégùn* of the *orisha* of their
> paternal family. If they are married, their husband's

Attributes of Ochún, the Virgin of Charity of El Cobre

family *orisha* is inherited by their children. To some
extent, the wives are outsiders in their husband's family. They are seen only as bearers of children and are
not fully integrated into their new household.

[. . .] Sometimes, for reasons indicated by divination, an individual may, while still retaining his affili-
ation to the family *orisha* cult, be required to join the
cult of another deity. For example, that of his wife if
she dies, or the cult of any other deity deemed necessary for certain situations such as illness, difficulty
producing an heir, or protection from specific or
unspecified threats. In such cases, the person becomes
more directly involved in the practice of a personal
cult.

One of the characteristics of the *orisha* religion is
its spirit of tolerance and the absence of any prose-
lytism. The reason and justification for this lie in the
nature of the cults and the fact that membership of
each cult is normally limited to members of certain
families.

Santería, more correctly known as the Regla de Ocha, has a
diverse pantheon of deities. They must be kept happy and satis-
fied on a regular basis with festive ceremonies. Respectful worship of the orishas through devotion, feeding and the ritual obser-
vance of all the important dates of the Santería liturgy is essential for those who practice the religion.

It is in Havana and Matanzas that the religion of the Yoruba or
the Lucumí—the popular and arbitrary name for those groups,
which may derive from the supposed port of Ulkami or Lucumí
in southern Nigeria—has the greatest hold on the population. The
rituals, music, symbolism and also the rich mythology and
hagiography attest to the complexity of the system. The cult of
the saints, the worship of the orishas could have no more appro-

Fundamentos africanos (stones, receptacles for the deities, which embody divine powers). The tradition in Matanzas keeps the otanes in jicaras (bottle-gourds) and cazuelas (earthenware pots) as opposed to the more modern soperas.

priate name than that given by ordinary people to this widespread Afro-Cuban religion: Santería.

As with the Yoruba of Nigeria, the focus or foundation of Cuban Santería is the stone (*otá*) in which the magical properties of the powers (forces of nature or deities) are seated. These round, polished stones, usually found in rivers, are the receptacles for these deities and devotees should carry them with them, at least during the more important rituals.

The highest grade in the Santería or Regla de Ocha hierarchy is the *olúo*. Like the Roman emperors, he should be over sixty to ensure the maturity and depth of experience that will give him the level of intuition needed to interpret the future without having recourse to physical divination systems. But the grade of olúo is rare and has now almost died out in Cuba.

In the distant past, the olúos or olúwos were the paramount

chiefs of the babalawo community.[13] But this structure, inherited from the kingdom of Oyó, was gradually diluted, and now the olúo remains in the hierarchy as the most expert diviner. It is the olúo who has the last word during the divination rituals for determining the sign of the year, or *letra del año*. This is one of the principal functions of the Regla de Ocha and carries with it an element of public duty. The olúo is "the rightful owner of the secrets."

Nevertheless, it is actually the babalawo, in his role of diviner par excellence, who rules the practice of Santería.[14] He possesses the attributes granted by Orula, the god of divination, for the practice of divinatory rituals using the divining tray and chain known as *opele* or *okuele*.[15]

Once Santería had established itself in Cuba it was the babalawo who introduced the Ifa divination system, from which originated other systems, such as *diloggún*, similar in complexity and detail to Ifá divination.[16] Like many other features of Santería, the diloggún is a true product of transculturation in Cuba. That is why we maintain that, although of African origin, this religion is a national creation, a living and eloquent example of the African component that has so strongly influenced Cuban culture.

The *babalocha* or *iyalocha*—*santero* or *santera*—who correspond to the Brazilian *pãe* or *mãe de santo*—occupy an important position in the Santería hierarchy.[17] They are in charge of specific liturgies, one of which is divination using the diloggún shells. Almost every day, these cult leaders introduce both *aleyos* (semi-initiates) and initiated practitioners to Yoruba mythology and its accompanying rituals.

Their lives, which are totally dedicated to the Santería religion, revolve around the ritual worship of the saints. They are subject to the taboos and whims of the deities and to religious

*Babalawo with opón-Ifá (divining tray) and okpele (divining chain)
in traditional divining position on estera (straw mat)
with his back against the wall.*

customs that are linked closely to material existence. Illness, economic difficulties and romantic problems—everything seems to depend on the capricious designs of the orishas. Their prophecies or predictions are communicated through one of the three main divination systems of the Regla de Ocha: *obí*, which uses four pieces of coconut and is the most basic; diloggún; and the Ifá divining tray. The latter is the most prestigious but is no more efficacious than either of the other systems.

One must be an expert to consult one of these complicated systems. In fact, someone skilled in the use of diloggún is called an *oriaté*—a highly respected figure. Even cult leaders defer to him, especially when they need to unravel some mystery or sorcery that is affecting the lives of *aleyos* or practitioners.

The oriaté is also the master of ceremonies at the most important Santería rituals. He is an absolute authority where divination and initiatory rites are concerned. An oriaté must be a true mentor and be present at all the stages through which people must pass before and after receiving an orisha's powers, or when they become initiated into the religion as a fully fledged santero.

Divination is the focal point of Santería. Like the Greek Eleusian rites, Lucumí initiation ceremonies are ruled by the dictum of the gods. The Ifá divining tray is used to determine whether or not someone should receive the aché (divine grace) that will allow him to proceed along the lengthy liturgical continuum that typifies Santería.

Even the rituals of Santería are determined by the will of the orishas: the right to receive the *collares* and the warriors, or to become initiated and thus receive on one's head the saint who becomes one's father or mother. Without the decision of the orishas, without their consent, nothing can be accomplished in the life of the practitioner, certainly not the right to receive

*A santería altar to Yemayá, Obatalá, Ochún and Changó with statues
of their Catholic counterparts: the Virgin of Regla,
the Gracious Mother of God, the Virgin of Charity of El Cobre—
the patron saint of Cuba—and St. Barbara.*

certain religious attributes.

When the saints are received or seated on the head, they become new members of the home or temple house. They become its masters. Nothing can be done in the house without first consulting them using the divinatory systems, the *registro* or consultation that is a feature of this regla. The other members of the family and anyone who visits the house will show respect and deference to the saints and ancestors, who should be greeted each morning by the santero.

Each saint has an associated corpus of legends or *pwatakís*. These are collected in the *libretas*, the traditional notebooks of Santería. They are like manuals that shape and preserve the religious traditions that have been retained and passed down from generation to generation.

There are a number of religious feasts and ceremonies in Santería. The most striking are those dedicated to a particular saint. During these ceremonies, one can express feelings of joy and thankfulness to specific saints and feelings of dissatisfaction or disapproval toward others. The latter are sometimes communicated in the *cantos de puya*.[18]

There are also celebrations attended by large numbers of people. Anyone can participate, and the purpose is simply fun and entertainment. The Lucumí call them *bembé* or *wemilere*. During these secular celebrations, *batá* drums may not be played and *güiros* or *abwes*—musical instruments made from gourds—are used instead.[19] These are always accompanied by an iron instrument shaped like a bell without a clapper, called an *agogo*, or else by the metal part of a hoe.

Three batá drums are played during the sacred initiation ceremonies or ceremonies for the saints' birthdays: the *iyá* or mother, which is the biggest; the medium-sized *itótele*; and the *okónkolo*, which is the smallest one and has the highest tone. These drums are given food offerings because each one contains a numen or semigod which has a magical secret, *aña*, which may not be revealed by those who construct and play them.

At sunset the exhausting beat of the batá comes to an end. The drums are taken back to the sacred room (*igbodu*) and remain there until the next ceremony, which always takes place during the hours of daylight. Afterward abwes are played, and with no time restrictions, the sacred or semiprofane celebrations can continue until after midnight.

For the Yoruba, the cult of the sun is important. This may be why the batá drums are granted the honor of being played during the day. This may recall a former cult of the god Olorun, who is the sun itself, in a remote Yoruba past. The most important Lucumí liturgical sung or percussive repertoire is known as *oru*.

According to Fernando Ortiz, there are three specific and identifiable areas in the temples (*ilé orisha*). They are: the *igbodu*, *eya aranla* and *iban baló*. The first is the sacred room, the second is the living room of the house and the third is the patio where familiar forces are found, represented by ritual animals and plants.

The oru, a repertoire of songs with a fixed sequence, are performed alternately using drums in the sacred room, *moyubando*[20] or uttering *a cappella* invocations in the living room, or with drums and chorus in the patio. Almost all the oru begin with an invocation played on drums, which normally takes place in the sacred room. The first deity to be invoked is Eshu Elegguá, god of the roads and of the future, he who opens and closes all the doors and who symbolizes the crossroads. As the oru and the ceremony proceed, certain types of behavior, body language, and frenzied displays are brought on by external stimuli. The phe-

*Left to right: obi (pieces of coconut meat used for divination) and jicara
with fresh water for libation; coconut later used for spiritual cleansing;
resguardos (talismans) for protection;
Elegguá; diloggún cowries for divination;
Elegguá Allé (shell), Elegguá made of a conch shell.
All items are prepared to receive a blood offering—the coconut pieces are
used to divine before and after.*

nomenon of possession trance is one example of the latter. This
is common to all Afro-Cuban religions and is particularly important in Santería.

The person possessed receives a god, who mounts his "horse";
that is, he takes over the person's body and makes him perform
contortions and gestures portraying that particular god's character. The possessed person may also dance and sing, displaying an
extraordinary virtuosity but naturally always acting out the man-
nerisms of the god.

The gods come down onto the head of their *omós* (children)
and turn them into victims of their absolute will, obliging them
to perform involuntary actions. Over the years, this phenomenon
has been interpreted in a number of ways, but René Clouzot's
explanation is perhaps the most convincing. Clouzot has attempted to explain how this phenomenon resembles a type of condi-

tioned reflex that originates in the initiation ceremonies. It is true that possession occurs in response to an external stimulus. The individual is conditioned within a social milieu and reacts to its stimuli. Cases in which the person possessed is a foreigner or someone who has not had any contact with these religions are rare. When this happens, the result is a truly grotesque and imitative performance that is artificial and overdone.

Prior contact is essential for any instance of possession. Whoever is entitled to be possessed by a saint and who succeeds in convincingly representing his gestures and character, immediately attains a powerful position within the social group in which these religions are practiced. It is worth pointing out that this power has as much to do with religion as with the social pecking order.

Possession also implies a willingness to embody an archetype that is profoundly linked to the identity of the person who consciously decides to adopt the traits and attributes of the deity. Furthermore, possession frequently reveals a determination to become something different, to behave in a way that links the person possessed to his native culture. Like the stars, the external stimuli influence but do not oblige. The person possessed has a faith that turns him into the docile horse of the saint who wishes to take possession of him.

One of the most impressive ceremones is the day of the drum. This stands out from other ceremonies such as initiation, the *itutu* or funeral ceremonies, the *agwan* where food offerings are made to Babalú Ayé, the *pinaldo* where one becomes entitled to use sharpened instruments to kill four-legged animals and the *icofá* where a special power is received from Orula. The day of the drum is the day when the person who has become initiated or made the saint is presented to the batá drum, whose lord is

Set of batá drums

Changó. He dances before the drum in recognition of its significance within the cult. This complex ritual has some unusual features. It is one of the occasions when the largest number of people are gathered in the temple house for a ceremony.

The recent initiate is dressed in his ritual clothing and is presented to the public before members of his brotherhood. It is a
day full of uncertainty and surprises. It is the day when everyone
acknowledges him and expects that he will be possessed in order
to show that he really has been dedicated to his saint.

The deities of the Lucumí pantheon inhabit the sociological
body that is Santería. They are like its nutrient cells. We use the
term Lucumí rather than Yoruba to emphasize that these divinities have been transculturated and that they make up a hybrid

group of new entities, in spite of the fact that the original Yoruba elements still dominate.

During the spontaneous and natural syncretic process that began when the first African discovered correspondences between his deities and the Catholic saints, it was the Yoruba traits that determined the nature of this comparison. The Catholic Church, which at certain historical periods recognized only its own supremacy, repressed the black Africans, compelling them to produce extremely complex sociological phenomena when they syncretized their divinities with Catholic saints. Nevertheless, this give and take of elements and attributes did not alter the basic concepts that were transplanted from Africa.

Referring to this syncretism, the Mexican sociologist Carlos A. Echánove points out that:

> If Santería lacks a theory to explain the aforementioned syncretisms, it *does* have one for explaining the almost exclusive role of the saints. Santería has been forced to ask itself what happens with God, the one and only god of the Catholics, a fundamental dogma of the religion found in Cuba which was imposed on the African immigrants. The answer is: Olofi (also the name of the African Supreme Being), "he created the world which was initially inhabited only by the saints. Later he shared out his power among them (that power is *aché*) in such a way that he never has to intervene in human destiny. That is what the saints are for."
>
> This is why Olofi is rarely invoked in Santería ceremonies (he only gets a brief mention in some ritual litanies), while the orishas are invoked frequently.
>
> Once this problem is theoretically eliminated, Santería can devote itself fully to the exclusive cult of the saints. It is in fact they who direct both the super-

human cosmos and human destiny. Hence their
extraordinary importance. Now this control is to some
degree shared among them. The theory of Santería
attempts to define the limits of these spheres of activ-
ity, as we will see later. There are 17 or 18 saints but
fewer than half of them are regularly invoked or called
upon in Santería.

There has been much debate about the number of divinities
worshiped in Santería and about their importance or position in
the hierarchy. Nothing conclusive has emerged from this debate.
Samuel Johnson identified 405 deities in Nigeria, but there are
fewer than 30 in Cuba. What is certain is that the Yoruba pantheon has shrunk over time. Many saints who had cults in the
nineteenth century are today almost unknown to modern practitioners.

On the other hand, this demonstrates the involution that the
religion has recently undergone in Cuba. The current syncretisms
take place when elements from older deities split off and incorporate other elements from religions of Bantu origin or even from
Roman Catholicism. Deities that occupied an important position
in the Nigerian Yoruba pantheon, like Oddúa, for example, have
almost been lost in Cuba. Others that are not tutelary deities
attained a position of supremacy and are the most commonly
worshiped today. This process of loss and expansion is characteristic of the passage of elements from one culture to another.
It also illustrates the permeability of a religion obliged, for
both social and environmental reasons, to adapt itself to a new
setting.

For the Yoruba of Nigeria life is ruled by the will of the gods.
"The gods are willful and ornery," as Esteban Montejo observed.[21] Once those gods reached Cuban soil they carried with

Attributes of Changó, the god of fire, music and virility

them their system of values, their attributes and their characteristics. In addition, they adapted, or rather they were adapted by, humans. But, on the whole, they lost more than they gained.

As Fernando Ortiz has remarked, the Yoruba gods often recall those of the Greek pantheon. They have an extraordinarily rich hagiography. Their avatars, manifestations or *caminos* (ways) are so diverse and reflect such historical intensity that it would be almost impossible to attempt to explain the origin of those that are attributed to each deity.

These advocations or versions of the orisha's personality almost always correspond to the various historical stages through which they passed in their lives. These stages may be related to warlike clashes in which various cultures met and produced an intense syncretism. They may correspond to different regions of origin or to the period in a deity's life when he ruled a country and was then forced by war to go to another, where he attempted to establish his rule. They may reflect ritual observances and other events that have so far been little studied.

An important element of Santería theory is (as Echánove explains) the fact that the saints reveal themselves on certain occasions. For example, when a santero is being initiated or during the consecration of a priest or one of the cult ceremonies when it is common for the "saint" to come down into some of the faithful.

Once again this shows how directly connected to reality the Yoruba religion is and how close the *orishas* are to mankind. They are capable of expressing themselves through humans. When they assume the guise of mortals and speak through them, it is a lively and real dialogue that enables the gods of Santería to exercise a more absolute power over humans.

Let us now look at some of the main characteristics of the

most popular Lucumí deities worshiped in Cuba. These are: Elegguá, Ochosi, Oggún, Orula, Changó, Yemayá, Obbatalá, Oyá, Ochún and Babalú Ayé.

The list also includes other deities who are less important such as: Oba, Orisha Oko, Naná Burukú, the Ibbeyi, Inle, Aggayú Solá, Yegguá, Osaín and others.

Eshu-Elegguá is undeniably important. All the Lucumí ceremonies begin with an invocation to him, performed either by singing or knocking three times on a surface to ask his permission to start.

Elegguá has always occupied a privileged position. First, he is the master of the ways, and it is he who opens and closes them. He marks the crossroads and to a certain extent is the master of what is to come, the future. It is necessary to consult him first before any action one chooses to take in life, especially if it involves travel or an enterprise. An offering to a saint, whether money or simply food, must first be given to him.

He also represents gaiety, happiness and cheerfulness. He is fond of mischievous pranks, of playing games with believers. Yet at the same time he may torment them mercilessly and impose the most severe punishments on those who fail to carry out his intentions. He lives in a stone or a shell, the branch of a tree, in wooden dolls or in a pear-shaped figure made from a lump of cement or stone with shells for the eyes and mouth. This anthropomorphic object is frequently found in the homes of santeros. Sometimes it is hidden behind a curtain or a shawl, or it is simply replaced by a doll made of glazed or unfired pottery or porcelain.

Elegguá, Oggún and Ochosi form the trio of the warrior saints. The three always go around together. They live in a little house that believers place behind the front door, and they act as the

Representation of Elegguá

guardians of the house. One of his main roles is that of watchman, though, according to legend, he was originally a diviner who passed the divining tray over to Orula, who is its master today.

Argeliers León has written about this trickster and malicious saint:

> Elebwa [as he prefers to spell the name] offers the image for resolving the economic and social contradictions of the ordinary man of the people—whether these were slaves or those who sought refuge in these religions at earlier points in the country's history. Elebwa is powerful enough to open a pathway, that is, to remove the obstacles imposed by the dominant class in society on the dominated classes. Elebwa also protects believers and frees them from the burden placed on them by other demanding deities such as Orula and Obbatalá. With his elegant attire and his congenial manner at parties, Elebwa represents the mystical realization of the hopes of the dominated class. This is why Elebwa is so important in Cuban Santería.

He is identified with the Infant of Atocha, the Lonely Soul, St. Anthony of Padua and also with the miraculous St. Martin de Porres. As Echú, he has many caminos. He has a necklace of red and black beads, in the colors that represent him.

Teodoro Díaz Fabelo has written about Elegguá: "He rules over the four corners of the world, the center and all the ways; in such places he is always found in the form of Echú. He opens and closes all the ways and doors and abides only by his own completely arbitrary decisions. Destiny, chance, unforeseen events, oblivion, tragedy, good or bad luck, success in anything; even our own progress and hopes, all depend on Eleggúa and Echú."

He is without a doubt the most influential of the Lucumí saints who rule over our island.

Ochosi is also a warrior and is one of those deities about whom much is said but little is known of their history and attributes. He is an old orisha, and his place is at the door of the ilé.[22] He represents the hunt and, like Oggún, is an expert hunter. His symbols are the bow and arrow. His colors are dark lilac and green. He wears a cap made from tigerskin and carries a quiver made from the same skin. His dance is rich in mime portaying the hunt. He is the patron saint of jails. In popular speech, to bear "the sign of Ochosi" means to be on one's way to jail or that some problem with the law lies in store. It is also said that he was a magician and diviner in ancient Nigerian culture. According to the myths, he is the son of Yemayá and the brother of Inle, the herbalist and doctor par excellence. His counterpart in the Catholic religion is St. Norbert.

Oggún is one of the oldest orishas of the Yoruba pantheon. The greatest warrior of all and the brother of Changó, in myths he is always competing with him for the coquettish Ochún, goddess of love and sex. He beats Changó in the most bloody fights. He symbolizes primitive force and earthy energy. Like Eleggúa, he is sly and cunning, but he is more headstrong.

He is the god of ore, of anything made from iron, of the mountains Oggué or Oké and of work tools. His symbols are machetes, shovels, pickaxes, chains, hammers, keys and other iron objects. The *chivirikí* or *alawedde* is a collection of iron objects that is kept in the house and belongs to him.

In Cuba his Roman Catholic manifestation is St. Peter, because St. Peter holds the keys to the Kingdom of Heaven. His colors are purple and green, and his clothes consist mainly of

*Alagwedé or Chivirikí, the attributes of Oggún the warrior orisha,
consisting of a cauldron and items that represent allegorically
the work of the blacksmith and of the hunter*

mariwo, fibers from forest plants. His mimed dance, during which he brandishes the machete that he uses to destroy forests, can be indiscriminately aggressive, either a war dance or a work dance. He carries a leather bag over his shoulder. The beads of his necklace are all purple or bright red and purple.

He lives in the forest and has many caminos; but in temple houses he is represented by a cauldron containing all kinds of iron objects. Sometimes he is symbolized by a simple horseshoe or a spike from a railway track. A metalworker, he represents the forge and is the protector of blacksmiths and those who drive any vehicle consisting of iron parts such as trucks and trains.

According to Teodoro Fabelo, "the Yoruba ancients used Oggún to represent the period of transition from the culture of the superior nomadic hunters to that of sedentary farmers." Undoubtedly one of the most complex deities of Cuban Santería, along with Ochosi and Elegguá, he forms part of the trio of warrior orishas.

Orula, Orunla, Orúmila or **Ifá** are some of the names of the tutelary deity of the Cuban Santería pantheon. He is the owner of the Ifá divining tray and also represents the divining tray itself. As the lord of divination and master of all magical powers, according to the mythology he is able to use his okuele and his divining tray to predict people's futures. He is highly respected, but there is little dialogue with him as, like Olofi and Olorun, the Supreme Deity, that vital element that represents the sun or daylight, Orula does not mount. He establishes close relationships only with the babalao and with his *akpetebí* (assistant), who must be a daughter of Ochún.

He is wise, old and grumpy and wields unlimited power over the lives of the babalawo and his clients. He has an iron will and is given to making drastic decisions. He is one of the most popular orishas of Cuban Santería. There is a very extensive hagiography about him, mainly because he speaks through the divining tray and because his *oddu* (signs) always come true.

His Catholic counterpart is St. Francis of Assissi. His colors are green and yellow, and his necklace consists of alternating beads in these colors. For some practitioners, Orula is the rightful assistant of Olofi. This in part explains the controversy about divine genealogy that is typical of Santería. However, everyone acknowledges the wisdom and intuition of this deity, who appears in the form of an all-seeing and all-knowing elderly patriarch. Anyone wearing an *irdé* (bead bracelet) on the wrist is assumed to have received Orula's aché.

Changó is one of the most venerated saints of the cults of Yoruba origin in Cuba. For many people, he is the most powerful and important orisha. In Nigeria he always held a prominent position among the founders of the Yoruba kingdom. He was a heroic king of the land of Oyo. During his reign he won countless victories that enhanced his reputation as the greatest Alaafin of Oyo, a title given to the highest chiefs of that region for centuries.

According to Alan Burns, Changó was the fourth king of Oyo, a mythical king of the Yoruba. He was the father of the nation and an eponymous hero. All the legends confer on him epithets that represent him as a virile and warriorlike hero. He was a womanizer, pugnacious, hard-drinking, brave, fearless, adventurous, given to defiance and challenges, proud of his manly attractions and very conscious of his strength and virile beauty.

When believers utter his name, they rise from their seats in order to salute and revere him. He is the god of music, owner of the sacred batá drums and of thunder and lightning. He is a very violent orisha. His energy manifests itself when he mounts and makes his horses spin round and deal out hefty blows. The royal palm is his sanctuary, his throne and his lookout point. From the vantage point of his own home he acts as the patron of warriors, hunters and fishermen. His colors are red and white, and his necklace consists of alternating beads in these colors. The double-headed axe is his main attribute, though he also holds the *palo mambó*[23] in his left hand.

For santeros his manifestation as St. Barbara makes Changó a deity with an androgynous quality. But nothing can detract from his manly pride and his invincibility as a victorious warrior. A myth tells how, after becoming demoralized, he vanished in the midst of astonished tribespeople, without anyone ever knowing how. There was a great outcry on earth and, at the moment when he disappeared, a storm of unparalleled violence with thunder and flashes of lightning broke out over the villages. The people in the Yoruba villages were frightened and exclaimed: "Changó has turned into an orisha!" This simplified version of the myth describes the deification of a god who devotees believe was originally a mortal.

His mortal condition is also documented in a legend that tells how Changó, at one phase in his life, was said to have had a brass palace with stables for ten thousand horses and how, after fighting valiantly on earth, he went to live in heaven, from where he now reigns over the State, hunting, fishing and going forth to make war. Leo Frobenius says that Changó is a mythical figure. He is the grandson of Aggayú (the desert or the firmament) and is descended from Okiskischeée. His father is Orungan (midday) and his mother is Yemayá (the mother of the fishes). His favorite siblings are Dadá and Oggún and his closest friend is Orisha Oko. His wives are the rivers Oyá, Ochún and Oba.

Middle: Santa Barbara (Changó); Right: the Virgin of Regla (Yemayá)

Numerous legends offer varying versions of how he came to commit incest with his mother, Yemayá, despite being the second son born from the womb of the goddess of universal motherhood. As the champion of soldiers, he disowns the cowardly or pusillanimous son. A set of batá drums, a bright red flag, a tortoiseshell *atcheré*[24] and a piebald horse are some of the favorite possessions of this god. The ram is his favorite animal, though cockerels and bulls are also sacrificed to him.

He breathes flame from his mouth. As the story goes, when he was the leader of the Yoruba people, lightning originated when he swallowed fire and then blew it out of his mouth. He is both feared and adored.

In Nigeria the cult to Changó is deeply rooted and temples

have been built to the god of fire and music in a number of cities and smaller towns. His dances have mimes that are both warlike and erotic. The latter display an eroticism that borders on indecency.

The former soldier who was deified appears in almost all the Yoruba legends. In Cuba, where he is equated with the Catholic St. Barbara, he is the husband of Oyá—war, and also of the faithful Oba and the seductive Ochún. He is undoubtedly one of the tutelary deities of Cuban Santería.

Yemayá is the model of the universal mother. Her seven-layered skirts proclaim the birth of humankind and of the gods. She is, by analogy with the Greek pantheon, the goddess of universal motherhood. She is the queen of the sea and salt water. Her color is navy blue with flecks of white to symbolize the foam of the waves.

Her dances are lively and undulating like the waves of the sea. Some are stormy and wild, while others are calm and sensual as, for example, when she appears in the camino of Asesú. She is also the goddess of intelligence and reason. Her children tend to have harmonious and balanced personalities.

She is "as black as jet as the babalochas say." This is why she is equated with the Virgin of Regla.[25] But this is also because the Virgin looks out to sea over the bay.

Many legends tell of a diligent Yemayá who is kind to her children, and a peacemaker. One of her oddest caminos is that of Olokun, a deity in his own right who lives chained to the bottom of the sea. Anyone who catches a glimpse of him will immediately die. He is seen only in dreams, as a blue-and-white-striped mask covers his face.

The sister of Ochún and the favorite of all the orishas, Yemayá represents common sense and reason, but when she punishes she can be implacable.

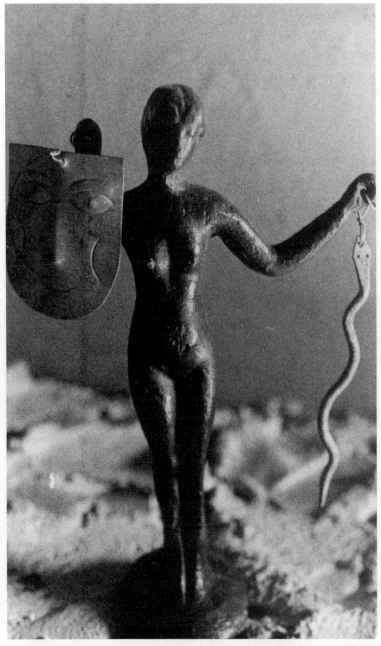

A Cuban representation of Yemayá Olokun

Her necklace is of seven beads of her color, blue, with seven alternating white beads. The majestic queen of the sea, she is extremely vain and haughty. She shelters her children in her skirts, feeds them and raises them with the absolute severity of a mother. Her emblems are a half moon, an anchor and a sun made from silver or a white metal. In the soup tureen where she lives is also found a life belt, seven *otá*—stones gathered on the seashore—and fans covered with cowrie shells, also one of her favorite attributes. In myths there is much mention of the incest she commits with her son Changó. In fact, Yemayá appears in some pwatakis as Changó's favorite wife.

Yemayá is a deity with a huge store of myths and legends. She is respected by all believers, so that when she appears at a *toque de santo*[26] and mounts her horse in the guise of either a haughty queen or a kind mother, everyone present will exclaim, "Oh, mío Yemayá!"

Obbatalá is an androgynous god in Cuba, because, like Changó, he can be represented in his syncretic form wearing female attire. He is Our Lady of Mercy. He has acquired special importance in the Regla de Ocha. Believers say that there are sixteen male and female Obbatalás. He is the god of purity and justice. He also represents truth, the immaculate and peace—this is why he is sometimes portrayed as a white dove—and wisdom.

The main camino of Obbatalá is Oddúa, the beginning and the end, or earth and heaven in Nigeria. According to Pierre Verger, this represents the earth-sea and earth-sky duality. Oddúa personifies the earth, its very center, its axis, while Obbatalá represents the sky. This duality is represented by two halves of a calabash: The upper half is heaven, Obbatalá and the lower half, the earth, is Oddúa.

The animals associated with Oddúa—a deity who has many

*Attributes of Yemayá, Yemayá Olokun, an avatar of Yemayá that dwells
at the bottom of the sea*

worshipers in Nigeria, such as the deer, elephant and even the dove—have passed over to Obbatalá's inventory as part of a curious process of transcultural borrowing.

This saint dresses all in white, his color. He is wrapped in cotton wool and kept in a high place. Sometimes people give him food offerings of meringue and coconut. In Santería temples, treading on the cotton wool is forbidden. This recalls the Christian prohibition on throwing away leftover communion bread. In Cuba, Obbatalá's caminos are very well defined: Oddúa, Oba Moro, Ochagriñán and Alláguna are the most important and well known.

In Santería liturgy he represents an essential quality. He represents the head, birth and anything that is sublime, very pure and clean. This is the reason that white is used in initiation rituals to symbolize something born pure like the *iyawó*, the new initiate who must spend a year dressed in white to show that he or she has just been born into a new life within the world of Santería.

Obbatalá is equated with Our Lady of Mercy or with the Blessed Sacrament of the Catholic religion. Obbatalá is the creator of the world, the beginning of everything. His symbolic implement is the *iruke*,[27] made from the hair of a piebald horse.

He has many attributes, including *aggogós*—handbells made of white metal, silver or silvery crowns, elephant tusks and so forth. Holy water belongs to him. According to some myths, he is the son of Olofi and his wife, Olodunlare.

Fernando Ortiz writes that Obbatalá is the celestial vault or the upper of the two halves into which the calabash of the world is divided. His necklace—*eleke*—is made from white beads. He is an extremely inflexible saint. His devotees must behave well and not utter blasphemies, get drunk, quarrel or undress in front of anyone. Closely linked to Orula and Changó, Obbatalá is the

king of the world and the principal head of Ocha. He is a tutelary
deity of the Cuban Lucumí Olympus.

Oyá is a stern deity who is directly associated with the phenomenon of death. She is equated with the Virgin of Candlemas
and also with St. Teresa of the Infant Jesus. She is mistress of
lightning and wind. She is the gatekeeper of the cemetery. She
protects and takes care of the dead and buries them in her
domain. It is said that her children and protégés are less subject
to the dangers of death than other people. Oyá is the rainbow and
is represented by its seven colors. The number seven is also her
symbolic number.

Only rarely does she come down, but when she descends into
the head of a human being she generally arrives with forceful,
haughty and violent gestures. She shakes her black horsehair
iruke in the air.

She is the sister of Yemayá, Ochún and Oba, and the four of
them fight over Changó. She sometimes carries him off and
accompanies him into battle, as she has a warriorlike nature.

According to the myths, Changó sometimes dresses in her
clothing to deceive the enemy and either elude or confront them
in disguise. His accomplice in matters relating to combat, Oyá
loves him but does not take care of him as Oba does; nor does she
seduce him as Ochún does. Instead she confronts him with her
defiant personality, which generally disconcerts him.

Her songs are serious and solemn but have a rare beauty. They
almost always invoke justice or peace. Her necklace is bright red
with black-and-white streaks. She is the owner of copper. In
Africa she is the goddess of the great Niger River and also rules
over hurricanes and lightning, which she is said to use to win bat-
tles. Like Changó, she inherited fire; when she gets angry she
also breathes flames from her mouth, but her fire is multicolored.

Object relating to Ochún Kolé, an avatar of Ochún,
the goddess of love and gold.

Oyá plays an important role in some Lucumí ceremonies—for example, the *itutu*, which is to appease and cool the dead. On the day the person dies, Oyá comes down and shakes her iruke in his face to show that she bids him welcome to the cemetery. The dead person should be cleansed before entering Oyá's kingdom.

Ochún-Kolé has all the womanly virtues: She is coquettish, beautiful, a flatterer, affectionate, obedient and hard-working. She is also a good dancer and very sensual and musical. She is one of the orishas about whose paternity there has been much speculation. She is described as a mulatto orisha, the mistress of rivers and fresh water, of gold and honey. One of the largest and mightiest tributaries of the River Niger bears her name.

She is considered the Lucumí Aphrodite. She is the goddess of carnal love and is equated with the patron saint of Cuba, the Charitable Virgin of El Cobre. As Ortiz has written, during Ochún's dances she demands oñí! Oñí! Or honey! Honey!, an aphrodisiac symbolizing the sweetness and deliciousness of the loving essence of life.

Her color is yellow, like that of the sandy riverbanks. She is summoned with a little brass bell that is rung in front of the yellow-and-white soup tureen in which she resides. Her favorite animal is the haughty and beautiful peacock.

As the staunch ally of the babalaos and Orula's assistant, she also has powers of divination, and according to the old blacks, she exercised these in times past.

In the legends there are numerous anecdotes about this deity and her turbulent love affair with Changó, whom she seduces and captivates with her talents as a capricious man-eater. Yeyé Cari, as she is also known, symbolizes the mulata of the colonial period or the typically Cuban sensual and stylish mulata. She has the elegance and charm of one who emerges victorious from Cupid's contests. She is proud and earthy, but in the camino of Iyammu she is calm, profound and serious. She lives on the sandy bottom of rivers, combing her hair, which mingles with algae and jellyfish.

Ochún Kolé, on the other hand, lives on the roofs or cornices of houses and converses with the turkey buzzard, her favorite bird. This Ochún watches over the others and is the eldest, some say. She embroiders and sews. She is always engaged in some domestic task. Now Panchágara really is "brash," an out-and-out prostitute. Her mission is to snatch other women's men and to that end she does not spare her resources of honey and gold, her erotic dances and sensuous hip movements.

Ochún is the patron of pregnant women; she is said to "look after bellies." She is a goddess with a powerful magnetism. She performs all kinds of miracles using the pumpkin that is her house and her lamp. It also has healing qualities. It is said that she always had plenty of cowry money and that she kept it in the sacred pumpkin along with her objects for witchcraft.

The shame she felt when her sister Yemayá surprised her having sex with her husband Orula the diviner, in the middle of a field of green pumpkins, means that her daughters loathe pumpkin and it may upset their stomachs. The liturgy has made it taboo. According to the pwatakí, Ochún was so ashamed that her daughters never ate pumpkin again.

There is no doubt about her importance in the Santería religion. She is one of the most venerated orishas and perhaps the one that has adapted most easily and naturally to Cuba. This is not only because of the syncretism linking the patron saint of Cuba with Ochún but also because, with her sensual grace and creole mischievousness, she represents Cuban womanhood.

Babalú Ayé,[28] St. Lazarus for the Catholics, the St. Lazarus of the crutches and the dogs (Taewo and Kainde), is, along with Changó and Ochún, one of the deities who has a deeply rooted cult in Cuba. Sometimes his mythology is rather confused. This is because, although Babalú Ayé now forms part of the Yoruba pantheon as a result of the cultural encounters that formed this culture, his true origin lies in Dahomey. More precisely, Babalú belongs to the Ewe-Fon (Adjá) culture or Arará, as it is popularly known in Cuba. This is a name as vague or arbitrary as that of Lucumí for the Yoruba.

He is the god of diseases; he performs miracles but is strict and inflexible toward those who do not obey him or who fail to honor the pledges made to him. According to the pwatakís he moved

Trono (altar) for St. Lazarus (Babalú Ayé)

around a lot and was a womanizer. It was on his travels that he contracted leprosy when he was already advanced in years. That is why he travels the world on crutches preaching respectability and upright conduct and receiving veneration from people of all nations.

He is accompanied by his faithful dogs. He is ulcerous and stooping and walks with difficulty, sounding his rattle and small iron weights to warn people of his coming so that they may flee and thus escape contagion.

He wears a coat made of jute with scraps of purple cloth. He carries a *ja*, a small broom made from the twigs of the shea butter palm. His special plant is the bitter broom that he uses to cleanse and purify the sick.[29] His collar is made of white beads streaked or striped with blue. He has a number of caminos such as Asoyí, Afreketé, Chapkuana and others. According to the genealogy of the Yoruba gods, Chapkuana appears to be the original or rightful god of smallpox.

While some gods inflict madness as a punishment, like Orula, or blindness, like Obbatalá, Babalú Ayé punishes and kills with gangrene, leprosy and smallpox. All the grains belong to him and to women, whom he is supposed to advise in their love affairs. He is also a god who deals with the dead. He is wise, like Orula and just like Obbatalá. Many believers maintain that he not only owns the wagon that carries the dead to the cemetery, like Charon with his boat, but also welcomes the dead to the cemetery grounds.

Babalú Ayé's messengers are mosquitoes and flies, carriers of epidemic and disease. Like the children of Ochún who may not eat pumpkin, his children are not allowed to eat roasted corn unless they first offer a portion to the orisha. Devotees of St. Lazarus or Babá are given to making pledges and performing the great sacrifice of flagellation. On the seventeenth of every month, they dress in sackcloth—the women in skirts and the men in trousers or shirts with gilded buttons. On December 17, his feast day, they fulfill a pledge that is now traditional in Havana. This involves a procession from distant points, on foot, on the knees, almost crawling along dragging stones or chains, to the sanctuary near the leper hospital in the village of El Rincón where he is worshiped. This sanctuary and the leper hospital have been the scene of the most spectacular acts of religious fanaticism ever seen in Cuba. Fortunately, these are becoming less common since the advent of free health care for all under socialism.

Babalú Ayé, St. Lazarus of the crutches, or Babá, as he is

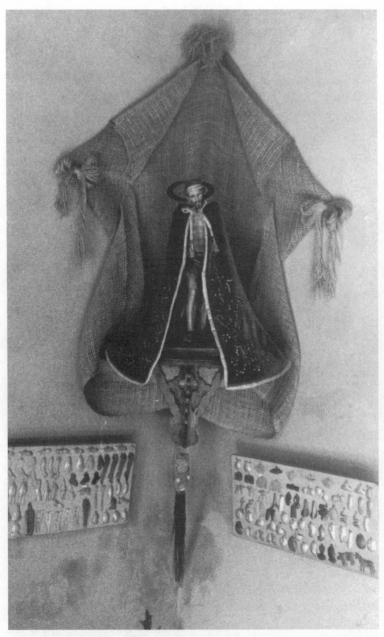

*St. Lazarus of the crutches, with an iruke (flywhisk used for cleansing) and
ex votos offered to Babalú Ayé in the Regla de Ocha for healing*

affectionately called by his devotees, has definitively inserted himself into the religious tradition of the Cuban people. It is now of little interest whether his origin is Arará or Yoruba. He is a transculturated deity and has become Cuban because his cult has undergone more modifications rather than preserving original characteristics that were brought to it during slavery times. A model of hybridity and fusion, even today Babalú Ayé exerts an influence that extends throughout the country. The syncretic process within Santería has been complex, and, although it took place on the island, its true origin is African. There the deities were already periodically undergoing symbiotic processes. This was mainly due to political and societal conditions.

The caminos often result from these exchanges, which lead a deity to lose importance and become a semigod or simply a lesser being. Sometimes these beings have the same name as the deity as well as a nickname; others have names that are completely different. In some cases the original deity disappears, remaining only as a camino with an unstable cult.

In Cuba we have observed how some deities that belong to various tribes or that came from neighboring territories tend to merge, while many others have gradually disappeared from the pantheon. There are a number of different theories about these caminos. One suggests that the caminos represent the different incarnations or stages during the lives of these deities as mortals. Closest to a historical view is that these entities are simply local manifestations associated with a specific geographical area and that they passed to a larger Yoruba group as the result of a sociopolitical exchange process. One tribe imposes its god on another, and vice versa. This may explain why transculturation leads some deities to gain importance, while others become either unimportant or less important.

Similarly, it must be recognized that the particular societal situations that confronted the slave in a new milieu, a new social and environmental reality, led to the rise of some deities that had not been preeminent in Africa. Others moved into the background in ritual practice.

No hierarchical arrangement of these deities based on their powers or attributes can ever be definitive. It is determined by historical moments and by the needs of believers. These will vary, depending on the particular way of life. Neverthless, life under slavery, with the tangible presence of the forest and the rivers, meant that deities associated with these places were still important. Agricultural work, economic necessity, precarious health, and traumatic sexual relations all influenced the retention of Yoruba deities such as Elegguá, Babalú Ayé, Changó, Ochún and forest gods, healers and sorcerers like Inle and Osaín.

In Santería, Oba, Orisha Oko, Naná Burukú, the Ibbeyi, Inle, Aggayú Solá, Yegguá, Osaín and others are objects of worship and are adored and respected although they are of secondary ritual importance. For believers, they are the repositories of magical and spiritual power, of the occult forces that the believers blindly obey. Some people believe that the deities that we have declared to be of secondary importance deserve a more prominent position. Our conclusions are based on their overall popularity and not on their importance for individual people. We know that for a child of Aggayú Solá or for the children of Inle or Orisha Oko, these deities occupy the main place in their religious life. It is a simply a question of numbers and not of their liturgical importance.

Oba is known as the loyal and obedient wife of Changó. She cut off her ears in a gruesome love sacrifice so that he could eat them with *amalá* (yam porridge). Loyal, domesticated and

Attributes of Orisha Oko, St. Isidore of farmers,
the god of fieldwork and agriculture.

industrious, she is a quiet and melancholy orisha. She does not dance or sing because she does not mount. Her Catholic counterpart is St. Rita, and she is the sister of Ochún and Oyá. The flamboyant tree belongs to her. **Orisha Oko** is the god of agriculture, the patron of farmers and countrymen. He also does not dance because he does not mount. Thus he does not have any particular mime, and it is hard to give a definite form to him. He is the lord of tilled land. He lives in the rooftops and talks to eagles and vultures. His Catholic counterpart is St. Isidore.

Little is known about **Naná Burukú**. He is an old and highly respected saint who cares for the sick and is "the mother of the St. Lazaruses." He is said to be the patron of the elderly. His Catholic counterpart is the Virgin of Mount Carmel. It is necessary to give him many offerings and to treat him gently, as he is very old and everything bothers him. It is assumed that he is of Ewe origin, and some people in Santiago syncretize him with St. Aemilius. His cult in Cuba is very small.

The **Ibbeyi**, transculturated into Sts. Damian and Cosmas, are twins. They are the patrons of children and are themselves children. Sons of Changó, they triumph effortlessly. Their fights involve childlike cunning and clever tricks. They are greedy and love sweet things and palm wine. They get up to all sorts of escapades. Obbatalá spoils them a great deal. Like their father Changó, they dress in red and white.

Inle, or St. Raphael, is the land itself; a bush doctor and expert healer. He can be a peasant or a fisherman. Sometimes he is equated with St. Ambrose. Coral and jet are his favorite stones.

Aggayú Solá is the acknowledged father of Changó, though, as every santero has "a little book,"[30] some maintain that he is actually the brother of the god of war and fire. He represents the globe. He is the Catholic St. Christopher. He has the gift of strength, which is why he is the patron of dock workers. They say that he is the lord of the immense forests and of the most powerful plants in them.

Yegguá is a female orisha. A chaste virgin, she is dressed in light colors, pinks or whites. She is very close to Oyá and Babalú Ayé because she is a deity who deals with the dead. She can be equated with Our Lady of Montserrat or the Virgin of the Helpless. She resembles the skeleton of a girl. Very few women are daughters of Yegguá. Those who are are banned from ever marrying and lead chaste and virginal lives. If they do not obey this command, they are permanently unhappy, according to Lucumí beliefs.

Osaín, the mysterious botanist, is the greatest herbalist, healer and lord of the mysteries of the forest. He has the most profound knowledge of plants and their healing qualities. He is lame, one-eyed and one-armed. The bottle gourd represents him, and he lives there suspended from the lintel of the ilé orisha. He can be identified with either St. Joseph, St. Benedict or St. Jerome.

Lydia Cabrera's informants equate him with St. Antony the Abbot and St. Sylvester. According to them "Osaín is St. Raymund Nonnatus[31] because Osaín is an orisha who has neither father nor mother. He appeared, he was not born."

Like Ochosi, he is an expert hunter, and he has exceptionally acute hearing despite having only one ear. The bottle gourd in which he lives is always found in temple houses (*casas de santo*).

There are other deities, perhaps with less status or less cultural significance in Cuba and in this complex world of Santería or the Regla de Ocha. Some of them are received in special ceremonies, along with their characteristic attributes. There are so many that it is not possible to describe them in this brief survey.

These orishas include, among others, Korin Koto, Boromú, Ayaó, Oggún Orí, Oggué, Ajá, Olosá, Aroni, Iroko and Oroina. Each one of these orishas adapted on Cuban soil. What this means is that some who were important deities in Nigeria did not remain so in Cuba. Others who were merely regional orishas acquired a greater importance in Cuba.

We have already seen how these deities became part of Cuba's cultural heritage. Some retained their original characteristics, while others lost importance and became intensely transculturated. But all of them went to make up that diverse pantheon of the Regla de Ocha that survives in Cuba.

Today new syncretic processes are causing the formation of a different ensemble, a much less stable and more complex creation. These recent phenomena simply indicate how society evolves toward new forms.

A process of horizontal growth has undermined the divine genealogical foundation of the Regla de Ocha. The former repositories of the liturgical mysteries are dead, and, as the result of a great spiritual vacuum, the religion has spread without having the necessary ritual guidance or knowledge accumulated since time immemorial. This new way of doing things has produced a chaotic and irreversible amalgam. Practitioners often get caught up in profound contradictions, but the religion of the orishas survives.

Of Santería, of the richness of its songs and dances, its mythology, only the purely aesthetic values will remain. The allegorical use of its philosophical and cosmogonic patterns will serve in artistic and literary creation.

In the near future, the deities will take the place occupied today by the gods of the Greek and Roman pantheons. They will be legendary figures who inspire writers and artists. The deep pool of African religions in Cuba, where those deities who live

Altar to the Virgin of Regla

on the surface or at the bottom still abound, will brim over more and more until one day we will hear only a dull tinkle and it will be Ochún's bracelets, or a feeble wheeze and it will be Changó breathing sacred fire from his mouth.

Cuban Santería is spreading throughout the world. Its ability to cross borders is due to the universal values that define it. *Moddú pue!*[32]

The Regla de Palo Monte

Tata Nkisi (priest of spirits) pointing at Sarabanda

DIFFUSION OF THE BANTU LANGUAGES

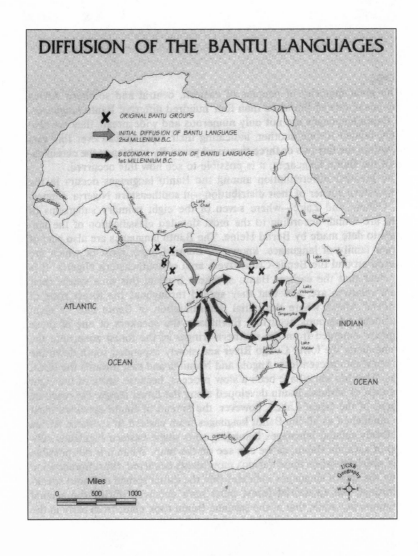

The African blacks who were cruelly transported to Cuba until 1873—the year when the last officially recorded slave ship entered a Cuban port—had diverse origins. They belonged to various language families and to quite distinct cultures. A large proportion of them came from the Congo region.

During the period of the abominable slave trade, it proved almost impossible to classify the cultural expressions of Bantu origin. The arbitrary label "Congo" was applied to many of these expressions. This was done to suggest rather than to affirm a relationship to the cultural and religious traditions that stemmed from the Bantu language family.

The Congos, as the slaves belonging to the groups from the Congo basin were called, came from one of the areas most devastated by the traffic in human beings during the slavery era. Many different tribes lived in this region that was covered in dense, abundant vegetation. Each had its own language, traditions and customs. On present-day maps of Africa one can find some of the names that are still used in Cuba to refer to one or other of the groups that came from the vast Congo territory.

Many old people still remember some of the names of the tribes or ethnic groups from which their ancestors were taken.

These names may vary from informant to informant. Their pro-
nunciation also varies, depending on the specific part of the
island where they were preserved and the distortions that resulted from the syncretic process. Nevertheless, the names
Briyumba, Kimbisa and Mayombe are recognized as the three
sources of culture and religion. These have become the principal
terms for the Congo religious cults of Bantu origin, at least in the
western part of the island. Other terms such as the "nations" of
Loango, Ngola, Benguela, Musundi, Kunalungo, Kabinde,
Basongo, Bakuba and Bushongo denote somewhat imprecise
places of origin. These terms were used by the practitioners of
the Congo religion and also in the *cabildos*,[33] where each group
was able to organize along separate lines. This is why it was possible to preserve ritual differences—less pronounced among
these groups than between the Yorubas and Congos—as well as
different musical styles and other defining features.

During the colonial period in Cuba there were many of these
"Congo cabildos." They were found mainly in the provinces of
Havana and Matanzas, in that vast expanse of the Llanura de
Colón. Economic reasons account for the large numbers of
Congo men in that area—the most important sugar plantations
were located in that region. Some of these cabildos were very
famous. Initiation rites, funeral ceremonies and purely recre-
ational public festivities could be held there, as well as a number
of other activities. One notable cabildo was that of the Congos
Reales. It was so famous and important that it had the most striking regalia and musical performances at the traditional Epiphany
festivities in Havana. On that day, it was only after this cabildo
appeared in the Plaza de Armas with its masquerades and *diablitos* (devil pranksters)[34] that the New Year Gift was distributed
from the Palace of the Captains General.

*Abakuá dance of the Ireme (diablito) performed by the
National Folk Dance Group of Cuba*

At the end of the eighteenth century, there was rapid growth in the number of cabildos. In 1799, by order of the Captain General, many were moved outside the city walls. This was to prevent their music, ceremonies and public displays from having an injurious effect on the population. At other times, especially during the periods leading up to the wars of independence, they were totally prohibited. It was alleged that they were institutions that encouraged witchcraft and impeded the march of civilization. All this seems to indicate that some cabildos actually were the venues for clandestine activities.

In Matanzas there were "Congo cabildos" of the Musundi and Loango. In Las Villas the Kunalungo or Kunalumbu were famous. The most important of those cabildos was in Sagua la Grande. Some of its former members are still alive today. What made the Congo cabildos so prominent was their lavish attire: starched shirts, top hats, frock coats, walking sticks, bracelets, arm rings and numerous other adornments.

According to Lydia Cabrera:

> Throughout the whole colonial period and for some time afterwards, there were numerous *cabildo*s of all nations in Havana, the smaller towns and provincial capitals. These included the Congos—Basongo, Mumbona, Bateke, Mundemba, Bakongo, Musabela, Kabinda, Bayaka, Benguela, Mondongo, Mayombe, Ngola and so forth. At the time, the decree of good governance of His Excellency the Count of Santa Clara, Ordenador and Captain General, which was published in the city of Havana on 28 January 1799, forced them to locate outside the city walls on account of their noisy ceremonies and wakes.
>
> My oldest informants were around when the *cabildo*s were still in operation and some used to frequent

Diablitos (dance of iremes for Day of the Kings)

them, "back in the 70s, when Napoleon lost power in
France and the Ten Years' War was going on here,"
says Bamboché, who wore the uniform of a *volun-
tario*.[35] Like others of his contemporaries, he hankered
after the colony, the *cabildos*, the Epiphany festivities,
abolished in 1884 "thanks to the *ñáñigos*"[36]—Carnival
and Holy Week. In the final decades of the 19th
century, these *cabildos*, where, as always and everywhere in Cuba, dances were held on Sundays, occupied houses on Monserrate, Maloja, San Nicolás,
Compostela and other streets in Havana, Regla,
Guanabacoa and Marianao. A few lasted up until the
beginning of the First World War. The Lucumí *cabildo*, Changó Terdún, had its days of glory but came to
a pitiful end. It lost its reputation and its funds were
stolen. What a mess! This would have been quite late
on, around 1927 or 28.

According to those elders, the *cabildo* of the
Congos Reales was very prestigious and managed to
amass considerable funds. There were also important
cabildos in Santa Clara, Sancti Spiritus, Remedios,
Sagua and Santiago de Cuba. We reproduce here related information that was collected and recorded on a
card:

That was the true style of the Congos from Ntótila,
a real Congo kingdom with a King, a Queen, court
and vassals. Everything was done there in an orderly
and honorable fashion. This is why the Congo *cabildo*
was called a kingdom. The festivities were exceeding-
ly good, the best; no expense was spared on items of
luxury. The King wore a frock coat and a sword and
sat on a throne beside his Queen, surrounded by
courtiers. There they ruled in the African style. How
could any of these *taitas*[37] ever match up to a King or
his minister or deputy?

In a daguerrotype that belonged to Don Manuel

Pérez Beato, that great expert on our history and colonial customs, the King of the *Cabildo*, also called a *capataz*,[38] is wearing a frock coat trimmed with braid, shoes with buckles and a sash across his shoulder. Instead of a sword he carries a stick with a tassel. On his head is a three-cornered hat with feathers.[39]

The existence of the cabildos enabled the Congo cults to organize in a more unified way. Once the cabildos disappeared they were replaced by temple houses in which the different lines or tendencies of the amalgamated Congo traditions merged and became even more complex and imprecise. Here too began to appear that phenomenon typical of societies controlled by a shaman—in this case the Congo Father or Tata *Nganga*.[40] Each person operates independently or in accordance with the orally transmitted traditions of his ancestors. He adopts the religion and its values in an individualistic manner, relying on his own personal viewpoint and on the traditions of his family or clan. For this reason, it

The king of the cabildo.
Cromolithograph from a 19th-century cigar box label

*Firmas for a spell to pay back a
harmful deed*

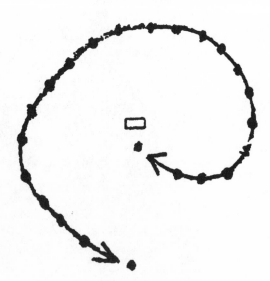

Firma for a cleansing ritual

became even more difficult to fit into a conventional classification scheme the mass of unformed and diffuse values that came from the Congo. Intermarriage between descendants of various Congo nations became more and more intensive and necessary. What mattered was to retain a conceptual unity. To that end, and in spite of the diversity of languages from the different nations, they attempted to create a common language. In this way a hybrid lexicon was developed consisting of assimilated Castilian Spanish and Congo words of Bantu origin—the common language family—though taken from its various dialects. No less permeable than other aspects of Congo culture, this language incorporated a huge number of loan words. Neologisms were coined to produce a type of Congo-derived broken Spanish that nowadays is used only as a ritual language.

The practitioners of these Congo cults did not remember the actual ethnic origins of their ancestors. Naturally this meant that they were also ignorant of the linguistic origins of words used in rituals. On the other hand, they tend to surround these words with a certain reticence or mystery. This demonstrates the ambiguous way they approach their special languages, their ignorance of precise origins of these, and their uncertainty about etymology.

This also happens with other more concrete aspects of the cult and liturgy and with the beings, gods and semigods of the Congo pantheon. No one element of the surviving Congo culture in our country can be defined in terms of its precise ethnographic origin. Instead, the ritual differences and the individual orientation of each *palero*—as practitioners of these *reglas*[41] or *palo* are called—are determined by the syncretisms that took place in Cuba. No single regla retains an orthodoxy vis-à-vis its geographical origin. None has been able to withstand the influence of external factors. On the contrary, the limited philosophical consistency of these cults and their animist and magical nature, rather than their mythological foundations—as was the case for the Lucumí—means that the Congo religions were more easily influenced than others. Even though the Congo religion is today the second most important African-derived religion in Cuba, in the period before the rise of the Yoruba religion the Congo sphere of influence extended across the island from the most impenetrable regions of Pinar del Río to the mountains of Sierra Maestra.

The predominant Yoruba influence has conditioned the permeability of the Congo cults. This influence has had an impact on standards and styles within the cults. However, it has not led to the wholesale or automatic incorporation of Yoruba deities into Congo ritual, as some authors have suggested. The Congo gods and semigods—that is, the supernatural forces they worship—have absorbed elements and characteristics from the Yoruba deities while retaining their own body of stories, the origin of which is not Yoruba but identifiably Bantu. Those stories transport us back to the Congo, to its rivers, mountains, trees and animals.

Thus there exists a complete Congo hagiography that was preserved, first in the colonial cabildos and later in the temple houses. While not denying that there was an overwhelming Yoruba influence on the Congo pantheon, we must also recognise that the Congo gods have distinct and authentic attributes.

The fragile and tractable nature of these sects allows any of their numerous followers to introduce into them their own individual forms and features. This process of give-and-take means that some elements were lost and not replaced. Transculturation had the effect of transforming the original expressive forms. In the process, attributes, dress, rituals, adornments, beads, decorated masks, carvings and countless liturgical objects were completely lost. The slave trade itself forced a change on the social and religious structures of the cults of Bantu origin. Many attributes lost their original informative or allegorical function and today survive only as decorative objects.

The flexibility of the religious beliefs, together with their remote and imprecise origins, awakened an imagination that is less dogmatic, more fanciful and creative than that of the Yoruba. This imagination and creativity allowed intensive syncretic processes to emerge in the Congo sects. We can affirm that nowadays the processes of syncretism are most intense among the Congo sects in our country. This is clearly due to the essentially tractable nature of the Reglas Congas.

Nevertheless, according to Esteban Montejo:

> I knew about two African religions in the barracoons, the Lucumí and the Conga. The Conga was the more important. At Flor de Sagua it was well known because the witches put spells on people. They gained the trust of all the slaves with their fortune-telling. I came to know the older blacks more after Abolition.
>
> But at Flor de Sagua I remember the chicherekú. The chicherekú was a little Congo man. He didn't speak Spanish. He was a small man with a big head who went running through the barracoons. He would jump up and land on your back. I seen it many times. I heard him squeal like a guinea pig. That's a fact, and even in the Porfuerza sugarmill, up to a few years ago, there was one who ran around that way. People used to run away from him because they said he was the devil himself and was allied with mayombe and with death. You couldn't play with chicherekú because it was dangerous. As for me, in truth, I don't like to talk much about him because I haven't seen him again, and if by happenstance . . . well, devil take it!

For the work of the Congo religion they used the dead and animals. They called the dead nkise and snakes majases, or emboba. They prepared cazuelas and everything, and that's where the secret to make hexes was. They were called ngangas. All the Congos had their ngangas for mayombe. The ngangas had to work with the sun. Because he has always been the intelligence and the strength of men. As the moon is for women. But the sun is more important because he gives life to the moon. The Congos worked with the sun almost every day. When they had a problem with some person, they followed that person along any path and gathered up the dirt they walked on. They saved it and put it in the nganga or in a secret little corner. As the sun went down, the life of the person would leave him. And at sunset the person was quite dead. I say this because it happens that I seen it a lot during slave times.[42]

From a sociological point of view, there is little that can be said about the Congo way of life or character. There has been a great deal of absurd speculation. In the last century it may have been possible to claim that they were "happy and hardworking," as an informant of Lydia Cabrera puts it, or "useless and lazy," as Captain Alexander asserts: "It was not only the Congos in rural areas who were accused of being lazy. 'In Havana,' writes Captain Alexander in the early part of the last century, 'rich families owned many useless and lazy slaves who had very little to do. They are just as idle as their masters and ten times as lethargic. They drink, gamble and are notorious in the city for being murderers.' He adds that many do as they please with their owners."[43]

Who can make unconditional statements about such a contro-

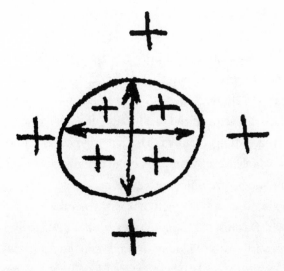

Firma for waging war

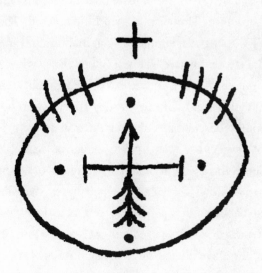

Firma for seeking a quarrel

versial issue? How can we go on repeating these subjective and unscientific generalizations? Is it likely that all the Congos were the same if they came from different tribal groups and if they had different customs and languages? The Congos were never a uniform nation. Although they stem from a common language family, those who were seized and brought to Cuba to work as slaves had distinguishing features. The heterogeneous nature of these groups, which were widely distributed across the island to work on plantations growing coffee, minor crops and sugar cane, makes it hard to sustain such reckless generalizations about their character. Or must the Congos always be the peaceable ones, the Lucumí warlike, the Mandingos predominantly runaways and the Carabalís thrifty and conservative? What light do these stereotypes throw on their Creole descendants, who are fully integrated into the national identity? Only shadows and more shadows.

The cultures of Congo origin that survive in our country have their own characteristics—philosophical, religious and relating to family structure. These have been little studied. Their worldview reveals a singular animistic imagination, and the customs and rituals are distinctive. This is clear. But, with respect to Congo origin, now quite obscure for its apparent descendants, who could claim that their present-day lifestyle differs radically from that of the descendants of other African ethnic groups? One should not forget that many practitioners of Santería are also paleros. This hybrid way of practicing religion, or as some call it, "santo cruzao" (crossed saint), demonstrates the very natural fusion that occurred spontaneously in Cuba, bringing together elements from various imported cultural expressions. The Tower of Babel of the slave plantations and sugar mills of the nineteenth century favored this exchange of resources. In a similar way, new styles and elements from spiritism and Roman Catholicism also

*Firma for performing good works and also
representing the good ncuyo*

Firma for Lucero

Firma for a priest of Palo Monte

flowed into and enriched the island's Congo sects.

While it is almost impossible to make the Cuban religious structure fit a rigid scheme, we can at least approximate an objective overview of a reality that, though always changing, is more or less accepted.

The names of some of the so-called nations (*tierras*)[44] are used to denote specific ritual tendencies within the Congo religion. These tierras are mentioned by practitioners but cannot be found on ethnographic maps of the Bantu region. They may refer to minor tribal groups in the Congo region of Africa, or they may simply be randomly chosen names of Bantu etymology that became adulterated in Cuba.

The amalgamation of rituals and the ethnic heterogeneity of the Cuban Congos is such that an attempt to decipher these names would be an almost heroic undertaking is if its futility did not make it absurd.

Lydia Cabrera gives a sense of this diversity:

> Like the Lucumís, the Congos prefixed the name of the tribe or region they came from with the generic term "Congo": Congo Babundo, Congo Musakamba, Congo Mpangu, Congo Bakongo, Congo Musundi, Congo Loembi, Congo Mbángala, Congo Kisenga, Congo Biringoyo, Congo Mbaka, Congo Kabinda, Congo Ntótila, Congo Bangá, Congo Musabele, Congo Mpemba, Congo Makuponko, Congo Kasamba, Congo Motembo, Congo Makuá, Congo Kumba, Congo Ngola, Congo Kisamba, Congo Nisanga, Congo Muluanda, Congo Lundé Butuá, Congo Nbanda, Congo Kisiamo etc.
>
> I have a copy of a document dated 1867–1869 from the National Archive in Havana that refers to the Nisanga:

"The free black Prío Morales, a Congo Nisanga, requests that the *Cabildo* be re-established for the purpose of holding discussions. The *capataces* and *matronas*[45] will be: First *Capataz*, Corrales and Second *Capataz*, Eduardo Cabrera, Third *Capataz* Ibáñez. First *Matrona* Mercedes Pulgarón, Second, Marta Tranquino and Third, Apolonia Domínguez. They have named as their patrons the Lord Jesus, Mary and Joseph. . . ."[46]

Our informants' Congo ancestors, who were once the most genuine repositories of these cultures, are dead. Their descendants' memories of them and of their stories are now so imaginative that examining them more closely is like entering a thorny tangle that is impossible to unravel. When speaking of their ancestors, everyone questioned refers to customs and ways of practicing the religion that bear little resemblance to the forms of today. The ancestors, as patriarchs, controlled the truth and preserved the foundation, but their descendants have transformed that truth and disturbed the foundation. Everyone follows the example of his Tata Nganga ancestors and criticizes the other groups, arguing simply that this is not how so-and-so said it should be done and that their particular ancestor was the custodian of the absolute truth. Almost all claim unique qualities for their Nganga, for the power concentrated within it, for the African elements with which it is charged, or simply because it is old. It is the Nganga that is the foundation of the Congo religion, its true center and focal point.

This diversity of opinion among the Congos means that their rituals and myths have acquired an openness and flexibility toward external influences that is absent in other religions such as those of the Yoruba, Arará or Iyesá. What follows is a possible structure for these sects, based on their origins and liturgical characteristics.

Many of these denominations originated long ago, and they reveal a syncretism that is also very remote. The form of the Congo rituals was preserved in the melting-pot created in the prisonlike dwellings of the slave barracoons, the cabildos and the temple houses or *munansos*. It became organized more or less in this way:

Regla Conga or **Regla de Palo, Palo Monte, Mayombe.**[47] This is the most comprehensive definition. The name refers to the sticks or branches from the forest that are used as a magical element in spells. This definition can include other Cuban Congo sects, and in fact it encompasses the magical rites of almost all the others. Mayombe or Palo Monte is one of the most widely known and popular rites. It is said to be used for evil; that is, it is "Jewish" rather than "Christian."[48] It is also said to resemble weeds and is associated with the dead. People use it when they wish to dabble in evil. Coal and gunpowder are used in bad works that are performed, preferably on Tuesdays, as that is the day of the Devil.

As Esteban Montejo explains:

> When a witch wanted to work evil stick-magic, he chose Tuesdays. Tuesdays are the devil's days, that's why they are so evil. It seems that the devil had to choose a day, and he decided on that one. To tell the truth each time I hear that word, Tuesday, just that, Tuesday, I go prickly inside. I feel the devil in person. If they were going to prepare a mean cazuela de mayombe, they did it on Tuesday. It had more power that way. It was made with beef, bones of Christians, shin bones mainly. Shin bones are good for the evil curse.

Then it was taken to an ant hill and was buried there. On Tuesdays always.

It was left in the ant hill for two or three weeks. One day, also a Tuesday, it had to be dug up. That was when they swore an oath that meant saying to the prenda, "I will do evil and do your bidding." That oath was spoken at twelve o'clock midnight, which is the devil's hour, and what the Congo swore became a contract with the devil. In a pact with the Congo devil, the oath was no joke or a tall tale. It had to be done right. If not, a person could even die all of sudden.

There are a lot of people who die like that, without sickness. It's a punishment from the devil. After the oath is spoken, and the prenda dug up, it was taken to the house, placed in a corner, and other ingredients were put in it to nourish it. The offerings were Guinea pepper, garlic, and guaguao peppers, a dead man's skull, and a shin bone wrapped in a black cloth. That cloth wrapping was placed over the cazuela, and . . . take care, whoever happened to look in there! The cazuela when it first came into the house didn't work, but when all those offerings were put into it, the devil himself would be frightened. There was no spell it couldn't work. It's also true that the cazuela had its lightning stone and its vulture stone, which were nothing less than evil.

I [have] seen just about every kind of terrible hex done with that. It killed people, derailed trains, burned houses down, well. . . . When you hear talk of black magic you have to stay calm and be respectful. Respect is what opens doors to everything. That was how I learned about things.[49]

In mayombe, Kandiempembe, the devil incarnate, the *endoqui malo* (bad endoqui)[50] is the spirit of the dead and of murderers

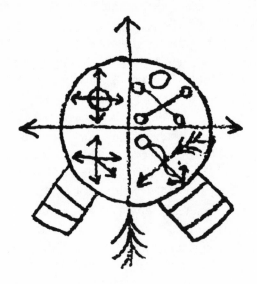

Firma for Nsasi Siete Rayos

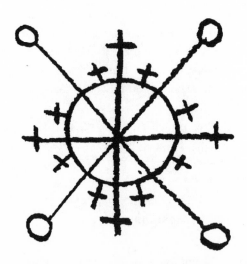

Firma for Prueba Fuerza (Test Strength)

and suicides. He is also the spirit of sorcerers. Mayombe can also be "Christian"—that is, used for doing good works and healing. Those attempting to decipher the cults' content and to devise a rigid structure are confronted by a confusing mess. This is due to the extremely loose nature of the surviving Congo religions, to the fertile imagination of practitioners and to the Congo openness to other cultures. Another factor is the defense mechanisms developed by practitioners who historically used esoteric codes and other measures to conceal the true nature of their activities from white nonbelievers.

If it is debatable whether, as Arthur Ramos affirmed many years ago, "the Bantu lacked a coherent cosmological system," it is nonetheless true that the myths, stories and legends that they managed to bring with them were subjected to all kinds of influences in the new environment. This transformed them into something different and created that language, rich in sayings and axioms, that is characteristic of the Congos. It also created a flexibility and, above all, a capacity for adapting to suit the times and for using external elements to enrich its own values.

It is easy, then, to see why some people regard mayombe as a "Jewish" sect in which black magic is practiced and whose members engage with the dead, while for others this religion is as salutary and constructive as any other cult group within the Bantu family.

Walterio Carbonell says that, for mayomberos, "The world is governed by a universal substance or spirit. This universal spirit has the capacity to materialise, that is, to take on the form of an animal, vegetable, mineral or human being. Everything takes its inspiration from the life-giving breath of Nsambi.[51] Animals and humans are endowed with an electrical charge. Some animals have a greater potentiality than others, for example, bulls, goats, majá-snakes and cockerels. The bull is used to feed the *palero's* nganga."

Referring to the sun—Olorun—that element which is also fundamental to Santería, he says, "The sun is the principal source of energy in the Universe. The *paleros* call it *Ntango*. A *mambo* or song to the sun reminds us of how important this heavenly body is for interpreting the existential world."[52]

The mayombero or palero works with earth, forest branches, stones, animals and all kinds of plants and objects. They assist him in the spells that he uses to save his clients. All the forces of nature, all living elements of nature—animate or personified— are found in Congo ceremonies. Like the gods or supernatural beings, these elements are the vehicles through which the palero

Prenda (seat of the spirits) of Palo Briyumba Congo with ntango (sun)
and upright crucifix. This Palo altar represents positive magic, referred to as
"cristiano" or "white" in terminology derived from Spanish.

can articulate his ritual language. In a distinctly animistic way, the palero uses nature to explain life. His oracle invokes the gods and natural forces in order to communicate ideas. In other words, the gods are explained by humans, and not vice versa. This is also expressed in a very eloquent African proverb: "Sambia speaks in the language of humans."

Briyumba is another popular regla among the paleros. Intended mainly for doing good, it has gained in popularity over the last twenty years. It is found mainly in the west of the island, in the provinces of Havana and Matanzas. The initiation rites and ceremonies for paying homage to the gods resemble those of the other sects.

Kimbisa is evidently an older sect. On the other hand, it is more mixed than some others, as it has incorporated a lot of elements from Western culture, spiritism and Roman Catholicism. Glasses of water, crucifixes and pictures of the Holy Sacrament are used. There are few practitioners of this sect still living.

Kimbisa is distinguished by its musical forms. One example is a secret drum called the *kinfuiti*, a sacred instrument, now rarely seen, which is played by friction and produces a strange dirgelike sound. Argeliers León describes the instrument in this way: "It is a drum fastened through the centre of the drumhead by a cord which passes inside and which is rhythmically rubbed using both hands. The drummer sits level with the drum, holding it between his legs with the head turned towards him. The drummer moistens his hands with a rather sticky liquid and when he rubs the drum the alternating friction produces a powerful and rhythmical rumbling. These rumbling instruments are generally secret. The *kinfuiti* itself is played behind a curtain."

The Regla Kimbisa is an obvious example of religious syncretism, of the blending of Spanish superstitions and popular

Firma for Sambia Nliri

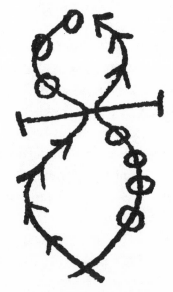

Firma for Remolino (Whirlwind)

Catholicism with elements from African rites. Andrés Petit, a popular religious personality of the colonial period, is credited with founding this regla under the name of Regla Kimbisa del Santo Cristo del Buen Viaje (Regla Kimbisa of the Holy Christ of the Good Journey).

These are, in essence, the main groups or tendencies of the Congo sects in Cuba, though others that derive from these can still be found today, one example of which is the Mayaca group, discovered in Oriente in the 1960s. These groups are less important and have a looser, more improvised structure. They are found in outlying areas and are named after gods or after the Congo *prendas*[53] that rule them or to which they are dedicated. They are associated with the specific powers concentrated in the nganga of an individual practitioner.

For some time now, we have observed how young and inexperienced paleros are contributing to the process of degeneration and disintegration of the sects. These fanatical practitioners call on the name of some prenda or allude to a forebear or old Tata Nganga who had a solid reputation. In this way, religious forms proliferate that are derived from the main Congo sects but lack deep roots, substance or a solid foundation. Often these smaller sects do not end up becoming cults, as they are unlikely to appeal to a wider social group. In any case, while they attempt to carry on time-honored and important Congo magical practices, they are, in fact, merely tattered remnants of those practices.

Music and Dance

Yuka dance on a Cuban plantation

There is no doubt that time has had the effect of simplifying many of the songs and much of the mimetic choreography of Congo dances such as the *maní* or the *yuka*. These dances were regular events in the slave barracoons on Sundays, the designated day of rest. They lifted the spirits of the slaves and released them from the fetters of a fatigue induced by workdays that sometimes exceeded twelve hours.

These dances are still performed on occasion in Cuba. They may be performed almost on a daily basis in the *palo* houses of any group, whether *briyumberos* or *kimbiseros*, at initiation ceremonies, feasts to honor a god, or simply to ensure that the prenda or nganga performs well.

These dances have a strongly collectivist character. Some, like the palo and yuka, are danced by couples; others, like the *macuta* and the *garabato*, are more of a free-for-all. However, all of them incorporate very expressive mime. The maní, for example, is performed only by men, though there have been cases of butch women dancing it. It resembles a boxing match in which blows are dealt with the elbow or the forearm. The opponent is always a member of a rival group, the opposite team. Nowadays, this dance has gone out of fashion.

According to Lydia Cabrera:

> People from the different African "nations" attended
> the *maní* and it was played all over the island. Like the
> appalling cock fights, it was popular with members of
> both races, "and it was not only the *ñanga bisu* (ordi-
> nary people) but also respectable whites who would
> go and watch the games." They bet money on the fists
> and aggressiveness of the "*maniceros*" in the same
> way as they bet on the spurs of fighting cocks. Many
> women, who were just as powerful as the men, took
> part in the game and they delivered punches which
> injured even the most skilful fighters.
>
> "In the Mercedes Carrillo sugar mill where Congos
> and Ararás played *maní*, Micaela Menéndez felled a
> huge fellow with a mighty blow."
>
> In Trinidad this sport was so popular that, so the
> story goes, a mayor and his daughter used to practice
> it. It was also popular in the province of Pinar del Río
> in the interior, and also in Santiago de Cuba and
> Oriente. A few years before I left Cuba, someone
> assured me that, even then, in a village in Vuelta
> Arriba, a group of black *guajiros* (peasants) would
> occasionally play *maní*. I did not have time to verify
> this.
>
> In Havana, where the memory of two famous
> *solares*[54] "El Palomar" and "Solar de Guinea" that
> were inhabited exclusively by Africans lives on in the
> coloured population, *maní* was played. The Solar de
> Guinea was very extensive and was situated on
> Marqués González between Zanja and San José.[55]

The macuta, an ancient dance of a religious and secret nature,
used to be performed in the *munanso bela*—a sacred room similar to the igbodú of the Lucumí. Two main characters took part in

the sequence: the king and the queen.

According to Lydia Cabrera's observations:

> Black women dressed in their best attended the *makuta*—my informants refer to them as either *yuka* or *makuta*. The *makuta* dancer wore an apron made from the skin of a wildcat or from buckskin. He wore little bells and rattles on his waist, shoulders and legs; hanging over his chest, a *gangarria*.[56] Using his whole body to mark the beat, he pursued the woman, who wore a very full skirt, and attempted to "vaccinate" her. He would suddenly stop in front of her and make a sudden forward thrust with his hips. They twisted and turned repeatedly and you could hear the *makuta* say "Tinguí tiko tikín."
>
> There were great *makuta* dancers—one of them was Villayo. His fame eventually eclipsed that of Pancho Becker. Here Nino de Cárdenas describes the

Makuta dance

band that livened up those "Kisomba Kía Ngóngo" or
Congo festivities:

It was made up of three drums. The *cachimbo*
which carries the beat, the *caja* which is more reso-
nant and makes a thumping noise, and the *mula* which
keeps time. The *koko* is positioned behind these three
drums, as is the *kinfuite*, a small harp-like drum with
a cord that is rubbed with a damp cloth, Kii Kii. . . .
This ensemble was called *makuta*. The small drum
was called *samlile matoko*, or the *alcahuete*.[57] A chorus of singers who also danced accompanied the
makuta. The person who led the singing was called
Gallo Makuta.[58] The dancers, both men and women,
answered the *Gallo* or *gallero*, who stood surrounded
by the chorus. It was a very lively dance.[59]

The palo had jerky hand movements, and the chest was thrust
forward as if it were gliding along. According to Fernando Ortiz,
the yuka was a secular and erotic fertility dance in which the
pelvises were bumped together to denote the consummation of
the sexual act, the possession of the female by the male.

The rhythms for dancing and singing are played on three types
of Congo drum: the *ngoma*—very similar to the *tumbadoras*[60]
with the same barrel shape; the *yuka* and the *macuta*, which are
accompanied by a *guateca*[61] or percussion iron. The *kinfuiti* is a
secret religious drum like the *ekue* of the Abakuá sects. The
ngoma are three drums "with straight staves in the form of an
inverted cone and a drumhead attached by nails. They are played
sitting down or with the drum tilted to one side." The three yuka
drums—the *caja*, the *mula* and the *cachimbo*—are accompanied
by a metal instrument made from the tip of a plow or plowshare
and by wrist maracas, as well as by a hollowed-out tree trunk
called a *guacára* that is played using two sticks.

According to Argeliers León:

For certain secular festivities, the groups of Bantu origin had drums known as *yuka*. In Cuba, these are
believed to be very ancient. They were used to accom-
pany the dance also known as *yuka* and the *maní* boxing matches. They were constructed in different sizes.
Some examples, preserved by the descendants of
those blacks, have an enormous diameter while others
are narrower. Three were always used: the biggest was
called *caja* by the Creoles, a name which derives from
the common name for the bass drum. The other two
are called *mula* and *cachimbo*. These three drums are
accompanied by percussion rhythms produced by tap-
ping a stick covered with a piece of brass, called a
guagua, and a ploughshare or any iron object that produces a strong sound capable of competing with the
stridency of the ensemble. The *caja* is played using
either a solid drumstick or the hand, or bare fists on
the drumhead which is made of skin from an ox's
neck. The drums are played standing astride the drum,
which is fastened to the drummer's belt by a large
ring. This is why they are said to be played by
"mounting" them. The *yuka* are made of leather
attached to the drum with nails. They are not sacred,
which is why they are not given sacrifices or food
offerings, nor does one need to be initiated to play
them. The *yuka* drums are very rustic. They consist of
a simple hollowed-out trunk. Certain fruit trees are
preferred as they are easy to hollow out, such as the
trunks of avocado or almond trees which are especially prized for making drums. The drumhead is fixed on
without too much attention to detail and sometimes is
not cut out in a circular shape but retains all the irreg-
ularities of the piece of leather. There was even a case,

Yuka dance on a Cuban plantation

albeit rare, where an entire goatskin was nailed to the
body of the drum. These Cuban drums are quite different from more typically Bantu examples, many of
which have neat decorations on the extra pieces of
leather that overhang. These are cut out carefully in
the shape of a circle and are neatly attached with nails.
These old drums are no longer played and are heard
only on rare occasions at special celebrations in rural
villages. A few old people can still remember the *yuka*
performances given in Havana in the early years of the
Republic.[62]

In the case of the macuta drums, two or three may be used, and
they are played using the bare hands. Sometimes, in order to
increase the stability of the drums, the macuteros tie them to their

belts with a cord. They are cylindrical and extremely wide, with staves and metal bands that are painted with the typical lines, shields or filigree markings of Congo symbolism.

To dance garabato[63] or palo, as this sliding and sometimes circular dance is known, a stick from a forest tree, generally the guava, is needed. This is called a *lungowa*. Old practitioners claim that the impact produced by striking these sticks together during the dance spreads the force of the earth and its magical and beneficial powers. This instrument has two functions, ritual and musical, but it is the former that takes us back to the time of the maroon *palenques*,[64] when the garabato was used for giving the signal to flee from slavehunters. The dull smack produced by striking together the garabatos accentuates the rhythm of the dance.

The Congo songs have short and simple melodies that are repeated over and over. They are less complex and melodically rich than those of the Yoruba, but they do have an incomparable rhythmical beauty. Lengthy recitatives are also typical of the Congo expressive forms. Many, like the songs themselves, have an explicit function. Some are to make the *prenda* perform, some are prayers for invoking supernatural forces, some salute important dignitaries—Tata Ngangas or Tata Nkisis—but certainly the most frank and improvisatory are the *macaguas* or *cantos de puya*. Described in nineteenth-century travelers' tales, these satirical songs, used by *paleros* for boasting or showing off, are full of innuendo and have highly improvised lyrics. For example, one song, "Switch It On and Turn It Off," refers to the most powerful Tata Nganga, who is as strong as dry corn. He can create light or extinguish it. Or "Pitiminí congo eá," which refers to an old quarrel between the Patuá Congos and the Congos Reales. The latter mocked the Patuá with gestures and jibes, while the

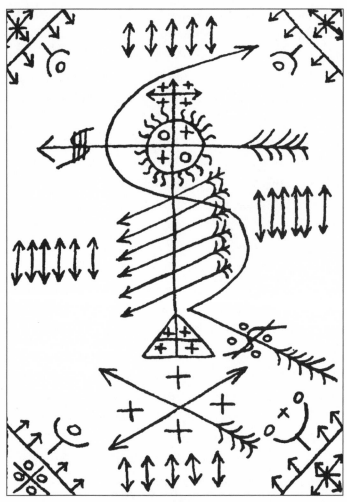

Firma for Sambia Mpungu

Patuá, who tended to be very short, challenged the Congos Reales by ducking and diving with great agility during the dance.

Like those of other peoples of African origin, the songs tend to be call and response, that is, they alternate between the soloist, called a *gallo*, and the choir members, who are called *vasallos* (vassals).

Dances, Firmas[65] and Magic

Dance in the interior of a Havana cabildo

The dances have features that are common to all African dances. They are performed in lines or circles, though recently new arrangements have appeared that apparently recall traditional dances. In one of these the dancers perform little jumps and move forward in a spiral pattern, making faces and waving colored handkerchiefs.

This simple choreography breaks down when the ceremony is held in a space that is too small and not very suitable. Then anarchy breaks out, and each dancer performs his steps in a freer style because of the need to restrict himself to a confined space.

During these dances, which sometimes reach absolute frenzy, the phenomenon of possession trance will often occur. When this happens the Congo receives into his body the spirit of a supernatural being and becomes a *perro de prenda*.[66] The energy of the dead person unleashes all its potential force on the perro, who apparently must contain the spirit until he can neutralize it with the help of the force and seductive powers of other people. This phenomenon acquires particular characteristics among the Congos.

The force that, according to believers, takes possession of the body and the will of a dancer or participant at the ceremony, may be regarded as a semigod. Its mimetic style is less well defined

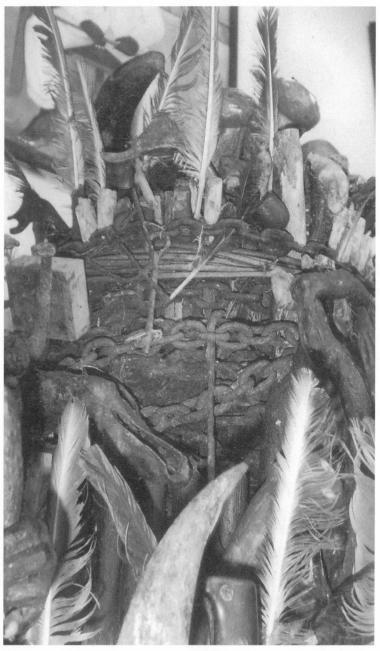

Sarabanda

than that of the Yoruba gods. Only in extremely rare cases does the perro perform a really varied mime. For the most part, when we are in the presence of a possessed Congo who claims to be mounted by Madre de Agua (Water Mother) or Sarabanda, what we are actually witnessing is a mimed portrayal of Yemayá or Ogún, their Lucumí counterparts. This is because the Congos preserved few of the mythological elements that would enable them to represent the characteristics of their supernatural beings.

The new forms prompted a process of exchange and syncretism that stimulated some of the old ones and eliminated others, though the *firmas*, the magic signs, remain. These display a remarkable number of complex and intricate features.

As Leovigildo López has pointed out:

> The *firmas* of the saints are used to perform "works." They play a very important part in this, so important that without the *firma,* nothing can be done. When a tata nganga intends to perform a work, after first asking permission of Zambia (God), the dead and Lucero, he then summons the saint of the cauldron by sketching the *firma,* as it is called. . . . If the *firma* is drawn with white chalk it is a *firma* intended for a good work, either healing someone or another type of work which does not involve harming anyone. However, if the *firma* is traced with black coal that alters things, because we are now dealing with a *firma* intended for a *trabajo judío*, that is, a work intended to cause harm.[67]

As we can see, the firma itself is a magical and dynamic element. It acquires an extraordinary importance each time it is used for individual ends. It is not only the supernatural forces that have a range of firmas; every priest bears his firma as means of iden-

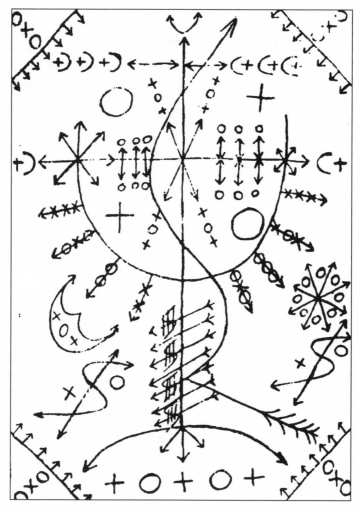

Firma for Madre Agua

tification, regardless of the rank or prestige of any member of a casa de palo.

The firmas are drawn in circular or straight lines on the ground, on walls, on the lids of cabinets, on cauldrons, on the door of the munanso bela, on the cloths tied diagonally across the chest, and on the head ties (*bandós*) worn by the men.

López adds: "It is said that no *briyumbero* ever draws his complete *firma*, because he would then risk someone using it to harm him. According to informants, the saint is found in the *firma*, that is, when a *briyumbero* draws a *firma*, the saint comes down into it. It seems reasonable to suppose that, by analogy, the *briyumbero* believes that when he traces his *firma*, he is potentially to be found in it. Therefore, whoever has the *firma* can control his person."

The artistic quality of these magical signs and their symbolism have inspired Cuban artists. They are used in their original form or in nationally acclaimed stylized works.

The most common elements in the firmas are simple; they are found in nature and in everyday life. Circles, lines, curves, arrows, crosses, horns, skulls, suns and moons are constants in these firmas, which the priests of the Regla de Palo have managed to preserve over the centuries for liturgical use.

Behind each firma lies a wealth of ideas that the slave trade could not destroy. The firmas are clearly part of the extensive repertoire of the lingua sacra that Africans brought to Cuba in order to express their ideas and beliefs.

The Congo liturgy is highly complex and contains forms that over time have created a very rich body of values. The core of this liturgy, its central focus, is the nganga. All powers are concentrated in the nganga, which is charged with animistic magic. Everything in the nganga, the nganga itself, is a magical and telluric force. Everything in the nganga has a level of energy, and this will vary according to the amount of time it has resided within it as part of its message.

For Lydia Cabrera, it is

> a spirit, a supernatural force, but also the receptacle itself, a clay pot, a three-legged iron cauldron, and in the now distant past, a bundle, a bag made from thick cloth or woven palm leaves in which are placed a human skull and bones, earth from the cemetery and the crossroads, sticks, plants, insects, bird and animal bones and other ingredients which make up an nganga. These provide the material foundation. Then there are the forces that the Father or Mother of the Nganga control and which carry out their orders. Nganga also means "dead person." Like the Nganga, the *Nkisi* or *Nkiso* is also the abode of a force, a spirit.[68]

These ngangas contain good and bad spirits, just like the sacred stones of the Lucumí. An old nganga dating from the time of the colony is a priceless trophy for the palero who owns it. It increases his prestige and assures him clientele. The nganga is the focus of the Congo cult, its core. Without the nganga there is no Regla de Palo, no Mayombe; "there is nothing." Within it are contained all the *mpungus*, the saints or supernatural beings. All the supernatural forces are condensed in the nganga, which is like a microcosm. Each tata and each believer is identified by his nganga. It is a large prenda, for prendas may simply be talismans or amulets and can be found within any object or thing or in trees, stones, shells, gourds, horns and so on.

Prendas are forces of secondary importance to the nganga. Many small groups of believers are formed around them. As

Esteban Montejo says:

The Congos said that a dead man shouldn't keep his
eyes open. They closed them for him with sperm, and
they stayed closed. If his eyes opened, it was a bad
sign. They always placed him face upward. I don't
know why but it appears to me it was the custom.
They put shoes and everything on the dead. If he was
a palero he had to leave his prenda to someone.
Usually when one of those Africans got sick, he made
it known who would inherit it. Then the prenda
remained in the hands of that person. Now, if that person couldn't carry on with the inherited prenda, he
had to throw it in the river so the current would carry
it off. Because anyone who didn't understand about an
inherited prenda would have his life all screwed up.
Those prendas could rebel on you like a son of a bitch.
They could kill anyone.

To prepare a prenda that works well, you have to
gather rocks, sticks, and bones. Those are the main
things. When lightning strikes, the Congo mark the
place well. Seven years went by, and they would
return there, dig a little, and take out a smooth rock for
the cazuela. Also the buzzard's stone was good for its
power. You had to be prepared for the moment when
the buzzard went to lay her eggs. She always laid two.
You would carefully take one of them and boil it in
salt water. After a short time you took it to the nest. It
was left there until the other egg hatched its chick.
Then the hard-boiled one, dry as it was, waited until
the buzzard went to the sea. Because she thought that
that egg would hatch a chick too. From the sea she
brought some magic. That magic was a tiny rough
stone that was put in the nest next to the egg. The tiny
stone contained a very strong witch. After a few hours

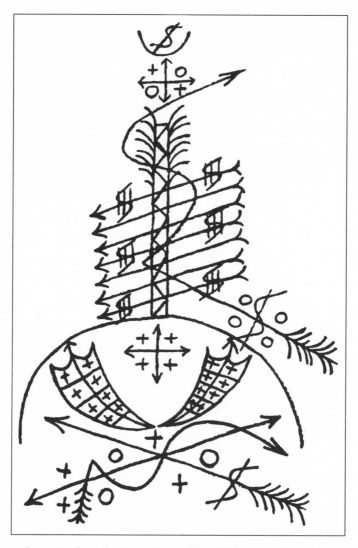

Composite firma for Brazo Fuerte, Tiembla Tierra and Siete Rayos

a chick came out of the hard-boiled egg. That was the honest truth. The prenda was prepared with that tiny stone. So this business was no game. One of those prendas couldn't be inherited by just anyone. That was the reason the Congos died so sad.[69]

For the divination ritual, the Congos use the *mpake* or *mpaka mensu*. This is a horn containing a number of ingredients that have magical powers. Its opening is covered with a mirror, usually of tinted glass. The sorcerer breathes on this mirror and interprets the figures that appear in the vapor. In addition to the mpaka, necklaces with amulets are used for divining.

Alcohol, tobacco and even gunpowder are used in these Regla de Palo divination rituals. For the Congos, divination is a supremely important element. To divine, to see the future, to organize life in a rapid and effective manner, is a priority in the cults of Bantu origin. Quick and reliable divination and the palero's efficacy in this métier guarantee his prestige in the Congo religion.

The Supernatural Beings of the Congos

Lucero (Elegguá in Ocha)

According to the theologians, God is transcendental. He created the world and mankind. The world bears his mark, his imprint. God explains and substantiates everything, but he is up above, lofty and inaccessible, and humans are down below. The forces of nature are found in forests, rivers, in the sea. This universal and inner God and the irrational need to reach him is also found among the Congo groups in Cuba. Paleros call this God Nsambi or Nzambi, Sambiampungo, or simply, Sambia. For the Congos, Nsambi is the Supreme Creator, like Olofi in Santería and Abasí for the Abakuá.

An informant of Lydia Cabrera says that "Sambia prepared the *menga*—blood—that flows through the veins, propels the body and gives it life. He breathed in through *nkutu*—the ear—the intelligence required for understanding."[70] There is no cult to Sambia, or should I say Nsambi or Sambiampungo—it is hard to please everyone as there are so many Congo terms to choose from—nor is he offered sacrifices or food. He lives in the abstract and is distant and impassive.

Next to Nsambi, initiates of the Regla de Palo worship the spirits of the ancestors, the dead—the most important—and the nature spirits that dwell in trees, rivers and the sea. These forces, or beings, as we choose to call them, have different names in different parts of the country or depending on the particular orientation of the cult.

It is impossible to establish an acceptable hierarchy for these supernatural beings (*mpungus*). These entities, which personify natural or supernatural forces, have numerous names and epithets. One could use a conventional hierarchical scheme to produce questionable lists of these beings, but these lists would not always reflect the ever-changing reality of the Congo rites. Nevertheless, we will attempt to establish an order of precedence for their relationships.

The most important entities of the Congo cults, irrespective of particular variations in attributes or powers or even names, are, after Nsambi the Creator, the following:

Tiembla Tierra (Earth Trembler). His name says it all. He is Lord of the Earth, of the Universe, whose reign extends to the four cardinal points and who carries out all Nsambi's designs and is his advocate and secretary. He is the Lucumí Obbatalá and the Gracious Virgin of the Catholic pantheon. Also known as Mama Kengue by mayomberos, this is an androgynous and omnipotent god. One may not invoke him often. He should be left in peace. Believers say that he is very touchy and flies into a rage if pestered with trivial requests.

Lucero Mundo, Khuyu, the Anima Sola of Purgatory,[71] the Infant of Prague or the Holy Child of Atocha. He opens and closes the ways. He is Lord of the Crossroads, Elegguá in Santería. For mayomberos he is found at the gates of the cemetery and is the guardian of the moon.

Sarabanda or Salabanda is strong and comes from the bush. He is the god of iron like Ogún in Santería and the Catholic St. Peter. Some Congos equate him with St. Michael the Archangel.

Lucero (Lord of the Crossroads)

It is commonly believed that Sarabanda is one of the most powerful beings in the mayombe cults. An nganga must have him inside it. He is closely linked with Siete Rayos, who gives him strength and helps him solve practitioners' problems. He works with the majá snake—*ñoca*—and is present in all the rituals of the Congo cults. Like most of the palo entities, he is a typical product of syncretism.

Siete Rayos (Seven Lightning Flashes) is Changó in Santería and the Catholic St. Barbara, and he is one of the most important gods of the Regla de Palo. Known as Munalungo by mayomberos, Ensasi, he works with fire and gunpowder. He is a warrior and is used for difficult and rapid magical works. Among kimbiseros he is known as Nkita, the name also given him by

Siete Rayos

some practitioners of mayombe.

Madre de Agua, Siete Sayas, Baluande (Mother of Water, Seven Skirts). This being is identified with the Holy Virgin of Regla. She is the mistress of the sea and of the mouths of rivers. Yemayá in Santería, she is common to all Congo sects and is much venerated. She has a stronger presence in the Cuban pantheon than most other supernatural forces. She symbolizes the unity of the world, everything that flows and universal motherhood.

Brazo Fuerte (Strongarm). Aggayú in Santería, he corresponds to the Catholic St. Christopher, who carries the globe on his back and wades across torrential rivers. Sometimes he is known as Cabo de guerra because he is a warlike and victorious being.

Pandilanga, Mpungo. He corresponds to Jesus of Nazareth, Jesus Christ Himself.

Chola, Mama Chola, Chola Awengue. Ochún, the Virgin of Charity of El Cobre, is much revered by the Congos. She is mistress of freshwater streams, rivers and gold. She is sometimes called Madre de Agua and confused with the mistress of the sea.

Tata Pansúa, Pata é llaga (Ulcerous Leg), **Tata Funde.** He is one of the most venerated entities and has many devotees throughout the island. He is equated with Babalú Ayé and St. Lazarus of the crutches, god of the sick and a miracle healer. Some call him Luleno or Asuano.

Centella (Lightning). Oyá in Santería, the Catholic Virgin of Candlemas is also the mistress of lightning flashes. Some equate her with St. Teresa of the Infant Jesus. Another of her names is Yaya Kengue, which is what mayomberos call her.

Lufo Kuyo. Ochosi, the Yoruba hunter god, the Catholic St. Norbert. He has few followers but is a prenda that, according to believers, both leads one into jail and gets one out of it.

Bután, Bután Keye is the faith healer or bush doctor. Osaín for santeros.

Kisimba, Mpungo, Kabonga. This is the wise Orula of the Yoruba, St. Francis of Assisi in the Catholic religion.

Mama Canata. An old entity who is identified with Our Lady of Mount Carmel.

Ntala and **Nsamba.** The Yoruba Ibbeyi, twins who are identified with Sts. Damian and Cosmas. They are believed to be the sons of Siete Rayos and Centella Endoqui.

Other mpungus appear with compound names that reflect the diversity of this pantheon that was re-created in Cuba. These mpungus, some of whom are considered to be prendas because they dwell in stones, shells or objects, both natural and man-made, have names like Endoqui Bueno (Good Endoqui) and Endoqui Malo (Bad Endoqui)—this may be an allusion to Elegguá and

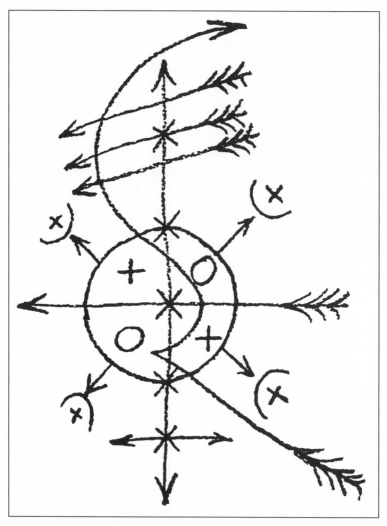

Composite firma for Madre Agua, Chola Wenguere,
Balúande, Buey Suelto, Lucero or Cuatro Vientos

Eshu, violent forces feared by the Congos. They include María Batalla (Mary Battle), Paso Fuerte (Strong Step), Buey Suelto (Wild Ox), Mariata Congo, Ma Fortuna (Mother Fortune), Ma Rosario (Mother Rosary), Zapatico Malacó (Malacó Little Shoe), Tengue Malo (Bad Tengue), Mariquilla (Little Maria). Then there are prendas used for doing evil, *prendas judías* with names like Infierno Mundo Camposanto (Hell World Cemetery), Infierno Barre Escoba (Hell Sweeper), Monte Oscuro (Dark Forest), Palo Prieto (Black Stick), Tormenta Endoqui Virao Endoqui (Endoqui Whirlwind), Saca Empeño (Debt Redeemer), Rabo e Nube (Whirlwind), Luna Nueva (New Moon), and others that, if mentioned here, would make this list interminable.

There is an interesting symbology that calls for a detailed study of these Congo beings that are linked to animals, natural forces and all kinds of objects. The animistic origin of these religions suggests that these beliefs may be linked to totemism. Using the appropriate tools, it would be interesting to analyze the relationship between a distant Bantu totemism and these groups of gods or beings and prendas.

How might one best investigate the relationship between totemic myths and religion? What is the origin of these beings? How were they shaped by the new environment into which they were brought? How do they relate to the intimate lives of believers? To what extent do they play a determining role in their daily lives? All of this remains to be studied.

Such studies are hampered by the amalgamated nature of the body of Congo beliefs and by the fact that they are constantly changing and adapting and are highly permeable. This is the greatest obstacle to any objective investigation. Any effort made in this direction is commendable, but all results must remain open to question. In this book, I have risked going over old

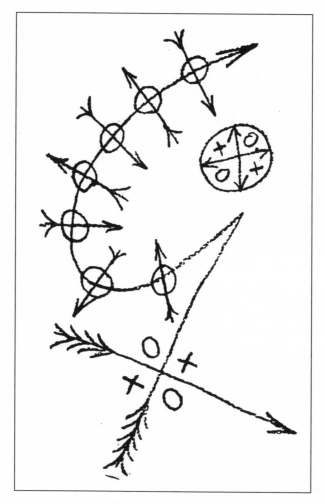

Firma for Sarabanda

ground, but I merely attempted to test out a slightly more organized structure for the Congo religion or Cuban Reglas Congas. The doors are open. Crossing the threshold is risky. We may meet endoqui forces fanning the flames beneath the cauldrons. But if we fail to take this step, we will in any case be consumed by far more dangerous flames, the flames of ignorance. Onward then, to clear away the thick undergrowth of the Congo forest.

In the Land of the Orishas

Carved wooden divining tray from Nigera

N igeria is a paradise. But every paradise has its hell. I
have never felt myself closer to that contrast, that duality, than in the land of the orishas. Nigeria has that
thing called *duende*, a strange type of magnetic quality with
which Federico García Lorca defined Granada. But Nigeria is
vast, horizontal and violent. Unlike Granada, Nigeria inhabits a
macrocosm that has its own peculiar magnetic energy.

If I ever decide to look for a haven, it will be beside the black
rock of Olumo in Abeokuta. The Ogun River and Yemayá's
stones are there.

"Well, Buka, I've asked you several times where the temple of
Yemayá is, and you haven't answered me."

"What temple? Yemayá lives at the bottom of that river, and no
one has ever seen her."

I had always believed that Yemayá represented the calm, vast
or dark and turbulent sea. She does represent this for practitioners of Santería in Cuba, but in Nigeria the goddess of motherhood
dwells at the bottom of the Ogun River and, like Olokun, does
not allow herself to be seen by anyone. Buka tells me that
Yemayá, the wife of Oggún, is Olokun's messenger and that she
can cure stomach ailments.

It is hard to tell how old Buka is. I ask him and, he replies in
clipped and guttural English. His answer is wise: he is a boy. That

is sufficient. After all, Western chronological age has no importance for the inhabitants of this region of the most densely populated country in Africa. In any case, I reckoned him to be about
eight or nine.

I climbed with Buka to the temple of Eggun, the spirit of the
ancestors and the god of longevity. I soon gave up counting the
polished black stone steps leading to the temple. Buka told me
that everyone who comes here counts them but that the total
always varies. There are always more, I thought. I truly did not
believe that I would ever reach the top, the lofty vantage point
from which one can make out the city of Abeokuta. The name
means "the city beneath the stones" or "the town at the foot of the
rocks."

Nigeria is a contradiction. The stones of Abeokuta could rival
those of Stonehenge in England or the Celtic dolmens, but the
tourist infrastructure in Yorubaland is limited. I was sure that it
had been weeks since a foreign visitor had climbed up to that
temple.

Buka, I said to myself, if you only knew that I never managed
to climb up to the Temple of the Sun at Teotihuacán. That I
stopped halfway on the first leg of the summit of the Great Wall
of China.

Buka's bare feet with their smooth salmon-colored soles
moved easily ahead and gave me the strength to climb the steps,
over four hundred, which led to the temple of Eggun.

Buka never doubted that I would reach the goal. Nor did I. I
might not have made it to the Pyramid of the Sun or the top of
the Chinese Wall, but I would reach the Eggun temple even if I
had to gasp for breath.

Nigeria was like a dream for me, and Olumo Rock was a chal-
lenge to be overcome. From time to time, Buka looked back, and
his black eyes, which seemed to possess an indomitable intensity, encouraged me to go on. My questions aroused Buka's curios-

ity. And he wanted coins, so he answered them, trying out his halting and sometimes unintelligible English.

Wole Soyinka, the Nigerian writer and Nobel laureate, had suggested to me shortly beforehand that I make this pilgrimage to Olumo. Ambassador Mazola and I were provided with a car and two aides-de-camp. I could understand Soyinka's pride in the city and its relics when I reached the summit of the temple. From there one could look out over Abeokuta, home of sacred orishas like Eggun, Oggún and Yemayá.

"Omó orisha?"[72] "Yes, I am a son of Oggún," Buka answered firmly. I did not meet a man in Abeokuta who was not a son of Oggún. I became aware then of the importance of regional cults, of the tribal structure of the Yoruba religion, of the power of lineage and of the intrinsically animistic meaning of the religion. There I was experiencing what I had previously only read about in books written by scholars and practitioners. I was in the heart of Nigeria.

Buka carried with him a supply of small sticks. I don't remember whether they tasted of mint or of eucalyptus. He gave me one, and I chewed it. Standing on Olumo Rock, a few steps from the Eggun temple, I had a strange but stimulating taste in my mouth. I could see the city, its markets and its industrious women from a height that gave me a necessary distance and made me feel somewhat exhilarated. Ambassador Mazola explained that the chlorophyll sticks were antiseptic and that Africans cleaned their teeth with them. That explained why I had seen such perfect white teeth in spite of the nutritional problems. Nigerians suffer from many diseases but never anything relating to the teeth. In the streets, in the markets or sitting in the doorways of their adobe and corrugated iron houses, they clean their teeth and create complicated hairstyles.

"Here it is." Buka pointed.

I breathed deeply and noisily, a breath that sought to express many things.

"Moddu pué," I said, and he understood me.

The ambassador and the aides-de-camp left me alone with Buka. With difficulty I reached the platform of the temple, a few steps from the entrance. At that moment there was a peal of thunder, but it was muffled and distant. Buka assured me that it never rained there. The dry earth spoke for itself.

The temple, like all Nigerian temples, is rustic and out in the open. There is only a gap in the rocks that allows access to a cave that one must stoop to enter, barefoot and with the head uncovered.

Children do not go in, because Eggun is the god of the ancestors and of longevity, and this is of little concern to children.

So I make my way alone into the interior of the cave. One can feel the humidity, and the pores begin to sweat a sticky liquid. The half light rescues from the gloom some esoteric designs on the dirt floor. These are made with cowries and dried seeds. I cannot decipher them. I can hear the distant laughter of Buka and my companions. They did not think I was going to enter the sacred chamber. As I am not used to walking barefoot, the dirt floor feels quite rough, and the small pebbles hurt my feet. The heat of the damp ground penetrates my skin.

"Agó!"[73] someone shouts at me from the back of the cave. "Agó!" I quickly reply. Little mounds of shells in the form of circles, little shells alongside the staffs of Eggun that lean against the wall. In the corners, offerings of unwrapped food stand beside improvised drains for the blackish-red liquid produced by the sacrifice of white-feathered creatures.

For the Yoruba, the Eggun staffs—*igguis*—are the incarnations of the spirits of the ancestors. The igguis are strewn about the chamber, leaning against the hot walls, laden with offerings.

The elderly priestesses—*arubas*—appear before me. I count seven within the cave. Three had remained outside. They address me in modern Yoruba, the dialect of Abeokuta. I understand some but not enough. "Moforibale! Moforibale!"[74] I say, and they answer enthusiastically.

They have been inside for hours. They prepare potions that are unfamiliar to me. I cannot see any herbs, just sticks and some reddish-white paste that I assume is made of tubers such as yam or African sweet potato.

I remain in silence. I try to avoid treading on the pots on the floor, some of which have holes in the middle.

The old *arubas* laugh, showing their white teeth, which haven't aged. I am immersed in a well of mystery, but I do not feel overwhelmed. On the contrary, I feel that this world also belongs to me. The old priestesses raise their arms in greeting. I receive this greeting like a blessing. They are daubed with *cascarilla*,[75] and their breasts are naked and drooping, like dry fruit. I do not spend too long inside. I have to continue to the temple of Oggún, the god of iron, a healer and the lord of Abeokuta. When I emerge, sweating and sticky, I see that Buka is holding a large stick in his hand. The old women who remained outside are laughing as well. We greet one another, and with the help of the stick I resume the climb. Accompanied by this retinue, I reach the summit. I ask Buka the name of the river that I can see below. He tells me it is the Ogun River and Yemayá lives in it with Olokun, the wife of Oddudúa, the creator of the Yoruba world.

I do not know how to say good-bye to Buka. Finally I do it in Lucumí. I hand him his stick and a few naira, the national currency. When we get into the car that will take us to the Oba's palace, I see Buka, son of Oggún, future priest of the caste of the god of war, running with his money toward a group of children who, like him, are barefoot. When the next stranger appears, Buka will abandon his games and climb Olumo Rock once again to earn a few more coins. Moddu pué, Buka!

The former Dahomey is now called Benin. This is a sonorous

Carved wooden divining trays from Nigeria

name that evokes an ancient empire of gold, masks and exquisite sculptured heads but a name that the inhabitants of this region of West Africa are not at all happy with. Dahomey, its former name, was the name of a king who had the power to sell his subjects, a king who, according to the Beninois, swallowed his people. But it is a traditional name, and in Africa, tradition is a sacred law.

Benin is a peaceful country, gentle. Its people belong to two main ethnic groups: the Mina[76] and the Fon. They live by cultivating crops such as yam, millet, cotton, pumpkins and various kinds of fruit. Benin pineapples are said to be the sweetest in Africa. I firmly believe it.

The coast is a sinuous, rose-colored swamp, lashed frequently by the Levantine wind, the harmattan, which, when it comes, covers everything with an irritating fine sand. When the harmattan comes, people must close the doors of the houses, go out as little as possible and prepare themselves for runny noses and allergies.

The capital, Cotonou, is a sprawling city, exposed to the tropical sun and to the rains from the north. It seems as if nothing ever happens in Cotonou. Its inhabitants swarm in the streets. They sell clothing hanging in long rows of clothes racks, coconut water, palm oil, liter bottles of gasoline, crafts and anything one can think of. But it is the pyramids of yam that catch the eye— huge yams with human shapes, piled up on makeshift tables or on tables covered in the loud fabrics that are also used for making clothes.

Cotonou is a peaceful swamp with the brashness of the tropics, where people appear to head toward one place: the market.

As in everywhere else in Africa, here the marketplace is the heart of the city. Vibrant and rich, it exposes itself shamelessly like a theater of assorted ethnicities, all on show in a remarkable piece of drama. It is not a Tower of Babel because everyone understands one another extremely well—French with muted notes of Fon, Mina or English, but, in short, a language for haggling.

In spite of everything, Cotonou is a modern city. Traditions are preserved there behind this modernity. The latest Peugeot models will never be able to compete with the wandering goats and the women dressed in batik with sacks of rice on their heads. Cotonou is one thing, Ouidah is quite another.

The inaugural meeting of the Scientific Steering Committee of the Slave Route, created by UNESCO, was held in Ouidah. I headed there, after various indescribable adventures, to take part as a member of the committee representing Cuba.

Ouidah has a sad history. For Africans it symbolizes ignominy and humiliation. The inhabitants of Ouidah were abducted, with the complicity of the tribal king, and taken in slave ships to America. The Portuguese and, in particular, Sousa, were responsible. But Ouidah and its inhabitants do not bear a grudge. The surname Sousa, that of the first trader in "pieces of ebony," sounds like an insult to the ears of the Ouidah people.[77] His descendants still live in Ouidah, but no one could say where. I imagine one of them, perhaps of a lighter complexion, lost among the mass of varied ethnicities of the little town.

Ouidah is a town of adobe and packed earth, of thatched or corrugated iron roofs, of dirt floors. It has the salty taste of all coastal towns, but it appears to be in the middle of meadowland. From Ouidah one cannot see the sea, but one can feel it like a malevolent force. A hot shower of sand falls suddenly on the streets and on the roofs of the market place—the holes, as they are called. A leaden sun burns the zinc roofs of the market's stalls, creating the effect of many mirrors and blinding us.

Ambulant vendors, mainly women, thrust ripe fruit, necklaces of colored beads, secondhand clothes and trinkets into the face of the visitor. The dust, and a sour stench mixed with orange and banana, turn them into the supreme deities of the city.

"The High Priest of vodun lives here," my UNESCO colleagues tell me.

I make time between the meetings to visit him along with Matthias, the Fon translator who is actually called Akandé. He is a man of medium height, a Christian with Western pretensions. Akandé prefers to call himself Matthias, though he admits that all his family practice vodun as well as consulting the Ifá divination system. Matthias tells me: "Ifá originated in Ketu, in the north of Benin, and then it came southward until it reached the land of the Yoruba and the Ibo. But it originated in Ketu, as did the babalaos."

Like Yoruba, Fon is a tonal language, which is why a word may have several meanings, depending on how the phonemes are accentuated. This language has a rhythmical musical quality with undertones of *marímbula*.[78] The High Priest of the voodooists had already been visited by another Cuban, the painter Mendive. There was a rudimentary mural by the artist on the walls of his temple-house, which is dedicated to the worship of Jebioso, the Dahomeyan god of fire; Changó in Cuban Santería.

Hounon, as this large, white-haired man is called, has a house with several rooms and courtyards. He has a black Peugeot, an electronic "three-in-one" sound system and all the essential comforts of the well-heeled.

Hounou must weigh a hundred kilos. The members of his household work hard. Each one sees to a different task. They cook yam, cassava and sweet potatoes. They prepare dolls containing various ingredients depending on the spells for which they are intended. They light candles to the *loas*.[79] Hounou receives us seated in a chair, the back of which is made from richly carved caoba, possibly Spanish Renaissance. The chair's upholstery is yellow and it is shabby, as are Hounou's hat and leather sandals. Hounou wears a white turban on his head and over it a wide-brimmed hat covered with silver paper. He reminds me of a character in the Los Marqueses *comparsa*,[80] but he has the characteristic dignity of a religious leader, a vodun Pope. He has been to Brazil and New York, and now he wants to come to Cuba because he knows that vodun is also practiced on the island. I extend a sincere verbal invitation, and he seems pleased. He asks me for a souvenir of Cuba, and I give him a coin with a single star: a royal escudo.[81] He wants to say a prayer for me, and I agree. He gives me a calabash of creamy, golden liquid to drink. It tastes of sulphur, old earth, damp. I really don't know how I manage to swallow it. The potion gives me the strength to inquire indiscreetly as to the ingredients. It is a potion of maize mixed with something else, who knows what? When I hand him the empty calabash I can see that there is a viscous coating on the bottom. He realizes this and says something to me in Fon that needs no translation. I nod my head and thank him for the drink.

I said good-bye to Hounou to the monotonous noise of a Beninois salsa band. That night during the closing ceremony, out in the open and accompanied by the din of the same band, the High Priest of vodun arrived in his black Peugeot, with his silver paper hat and two minders. He was so caught up in his role of religious leader that he did not recognize me among the many foreign visitors. His blue eyes of an elderly guru focused only on a point in infinity.

Hounou must certainly come to Cuba one day to spread his *aché*[82] among the Haitians of the island, accompanied by his retinue of loas and zombies of ancient Dahomey. The voices of Marrakesh seem faint and almost muted in comparison with the voices of Lagos. One of the biggest capital cities in Africa—Lagos—named thus by a Portuguese colonizer, is also a vast swamp. But it is more crowded and violent than Cotonou. Enclosed by tall coconut palms and dense woods surrounding the small lakes, the former capital of Nigeria is a city with a bourgeoisie of affluent businesspeople. Even the most modest of these merchants has a Mercedes Benz and races it through the paved streets, across the kilometer-long bridges and along the dirt roads with greater pride than if he were riding on an elephant. Clearly the Mercedes Benz has come to replace the majesty of these pachyderms.

In the Lagos region, the border between Benin and Nigeria is a seething mass of cars, many of them Mercedes. It is a border unlike any other, with police in khaki carrying batons and whips for driving away the ambulant traders from Benin. To cross this border illegally is the unattainable dream of many Beninois who wish to offer their wide range of products to a more profitable market. It is a horrifying scene, but that is how it is. Like startled hens, the vendors run backward with their loads on their heads. Only those who leave a coin in the hands of their ad hoc enemies manage to escape. What one had imagined to be a heterogeneous and multiethnic country is, in fact, two countries. The traveler becomes aware of this at the border. And it is not just a question of language but of culture and pace of life: Nigerian energy as opposed to Beninois lassitude.

We spend an hour crossing the border; a flat area pockmarked with puddles of foul-smelling water and stern looks. Here English dominates, a sonorous English with Yoruba phonetics and short, syncopated sentences. There is an air of agitation, of uncertainty and of violence at the entrance to the land of the orishas. A few meters from the border, on a deserted beach, Eshu is being worshipped and offerings are placed on circles of cowries in memory of the slaves who left from here for America. The officiants are greeted at the border posts with religious songs. Some return to Benin; others continue their journey to Lagos.

Once the immigration formalities have been dealt with, we prepare to cross the longest bridge in Africa, probably the longest in the world. Under the bridge are big lakes and the tributaries of great rivers dotted with small islands. Suddenly, as if emerging from the pages of a travel book, the city appears, with its giddy rhythm and dazzling colors.

A swarm of cars is crammed onto the bridge, and the street sellers appear once again to take advantage of the traffic jam, as this bottleneck, now characteristic of the city, is known. They besiege vehicles on both sides to push their wares. They are able to cover many meters in long strides, following the cars and offering anything from coconut water to digital watches, fabrics and fruit, all at bargain prices.

I know of no other city with such an abundance of things as Lagos. With prices that are cheap compared to the big cities of Europe, the goods on offer pile up in the small shops and in the hands of the vendors, because the purchasing power of Nigerians is fairly limited.

I will never forget the sight of a young woman with a child on her back, offering flour cakes and boiled corncobs, who ran behind the car until it reached the traffic lights. The young woman had been reducing the price of her goods, and at the finish line she almost gave them to us. This happens all the time. Even so, the vendors often return home carrying their entire load, having sold nothing.

Lagos is an overpopulated city. A large proportion of the Yoruba ethnic group live and work there. The Yoruba—almost twenty million people—are scattered throughout Nigeria. But it is in the southwest that this culture is dominant. Cities such as Lagos, Ife, Ibadan, Abeokuta, Oshogbo and Oyo, to mention but a few, have a very high concentration of Yorubas. Oddudúa, the founding father of the Yoruba nation, is the axis around which the world of the orishas turns.

I inquired everywhere about Oddudúa. Everyone gave the same answer: he was the first Oni of Ife, the owner of the ARE crown, symbol of absolute power. The Yoruba are the legitimate children of Oddudúa. I asked about the word Yoruba. No one could tell me its origin. What is certain is that the term is used widely to identify this people and their language. Some told me that the word Yoruba is of Hausa origin, that is, from the north of Nigeria, an Arabic word. I was none the wiser. I asked about the word Lucumí: few recognized the term. Some told me it had been a kingdom of the Oyo Empire. Others that it was the original name of the Yoruba and that Ulkami had been a place where slaves were sold and traded. Thus the name Lucumí is derived from Ulkami, that is, a metathesis of the word. What is known is that the term was coined in Cuba. Here it became the prevailing term and is still current.

I spent several days making discoveries and asking questions in the world of Oddudúa. The orishas of the Yoruba or Lucumí pantheon, the only system that has provided Cuban culture with an extremely rich repertoire of myths, appeared in my path at every turn: among the recesses of the Marina market, in the meandering Ogun River, or on the dark sands of Badagry.

Nothing more closely resembles a Havana solar than the recesses of Marina market. An overcrowded Havana solar but without the rowdy uproar that is more Andalusian than African, because Africans have more refined manners and are much quieter. Wiping their hands, washing their feet and faces in basins, the inhabitants of Lagos gather there to wait. The Muslims gather for the holy hour of Ramadan—at around five in the afternoon—or simply to sell their fabrics, food, magic powders and their unrivaled handicrafts, crafts that belong to a distant tradition, lost in the past of the Oyo or Benin Empire. They are distinguished by their disproportionate size and exaggerated shapes. The customer will not find antiques or museum pieces in these shops. Within the hot canvas and wooden stalls is packed a compact display of original pieces of extraordinary quality and beauty. They are not antiques but modern pieces, some deliberately aged, but made for the customer of the moment, for the tourist.

Diego Rivera rightly argued that although the pieces of pre-Columbian art in his collection were neither antiques nor unique, they were as authentic and valuable as the originals. This was because they were made by the hands of generations who had inherited an unprecedented artistic tradition. They were the same talents expressed in different eras. All they lacked was antiquity. The Marina market, or the Junkyard, as some people call the market where crafts and carved furniture are sold, displays many different examples of this talent, which is characteristic of Nigerians. Immersing oneself in this market is like entering a toyshop out of Lewis Carroll, a veritable wonderland.

I don't know whether the goatskin fan I bought is really a utilitarian object or a portable toy for performing conjuring tricks. The reader would need to see it.

I said that Nigeria was a paradise and that every paradise has its hell. The reader cannot imagine the sensations produced when one enters the vortex of Marina market. The stench rises from the puddles and the gray drains, from the narrow lanes crammed with works of art, batik fabric and heavily spiced food . . . it is indescribable. Mixed in with this is the smell of nutmeg and cinnamon, mint and vetiver, the sour sweat of the hides and the heavy aroma of the stews that are the fathers or perhaps the grandfathers of our broths and our *ajiaco,*[83] what the Nigerians call soul food. I have seen other markets elsewhere in the world, including Africa, but none more impressive than the Marina in Lagos. The word *Agó!*, like the sound of the Chinese cornet at the Santiago Carnival, imposes its high-pitched note on the mass of people that flood this place of meetings and of chaos. Young faces, full of vitality, women with children on their backs, old men reclining on large tins of fat, old women with portable furnaces on their heads cooking food, legless men dragging themselves along, crippled, blind and one-armed beggars . . . all of this evokes one of the busiest places in the world and one of the most brashly fascinating—Marina market in Lagos, Agó!

The Yoruba religious leader Majeobaje tells me that when Olofi created the world he brought together many powers and many forces among the peoples of the ancient kingdom of Oyo. It was not by chance that this kingdom attained such importance and had such a long reign. Olofi made everything that is beautiful and everything that is ugly, and he charged Oddudúa with founding the Yoruba nation. Oddudúa was the great builder. He used his hands to mold each of the beings that would inhabit this empire. But the world has two sides, Majeobaje tells me, indicating the palm and back of his hand. Majeobaje dresses in blue and wears heavy necklaces, also blue, and a leather pouch in which he keeps papers and business cards hangs from his slender neck. Majeobaje is young and has the most perfect teeth imaginable. He speaks correct English but greets me in Yoruba: "Ború boyé! Mforibale!"[84] He laughs loudly at my reply in Cuban Lucumí. He invites me into his home. I have to stoop to enter it. Once inside he asks me to say "Aché!" every time he invokes one of his deities, represented by pots scattered asymmetrically about the floor of his *ibodú*—the room of the orishas.

Majeobaje is one of the religious leaders of Olofin, one of the most respected throughout the Yoruba world. I tell him something of myself. Naturally he senses that I am eternally curious and that I have something in common with him. The parents of Esteban Montejo, the runaway slave, were Yorubas from Oyo. I tell him the story, and he is moved by it. He suggests that we should go to the beach to pray for him and to offer fruit to his spirit, that I should sponsor a drum ceremony in his honor. All these men, he tells me, have suffered greatly and will return to a better life in their homeland. The alien lands harmed them, and they will find peace only in their homeland. This is why they must be tempted with offerings.

I ask him if it is Yemayá who will see to this. But he doesn't answer. He simply reminds me that there is only one life, one on earth and the other, which is not in some abstract heaven but also here, with the orishas. When I go out into the as yet unpaved street, I see some children playing with cassava balls. I wonder whether Esteban Montejo, who died in Havana at the age of 113, has perhaps been reincarnated in one of them.

Majeobaje buys the fruit for me: two coconuts, bananas and a small, long pineapple, one of the very sweet ones from West Africa. He knows my time is limited, and he does not leave it until tomorrow. We make for the sea. We walk barefoot and in perfect communion along the sand which is the color of roasted maize. On the seashore, the religious leader improvises some beautiful prayers to Eshu-Eleggúa. He wraps the fruit in a white cloth and leaves it there for the waves to decide what to do with it. With only solidarity to steer them, the fruit will surely reach its destination. It will fulfill its mission.

"Agó!" I hear once again from Majeobaje's lips. "Agó, Iba e tonú tonú!"[85] When the ritual is concluded, Majeobaje and I sit down at a table beside the beach. I ask for coconut water and he for a rum and Coke. "Cuba Libre," I say—that is what the drink is called—but the name means nothing to him.

At my request he tells me more about Oddudúa and the two sides of the world. Majeobaje is a born storyteller. Car horns, motorcycle hooters and bicycle bells interrupt his story.

"A wedding?" I ask.

"No, a funeral."

We look behind us, and he is surprised by my expression. He explains: "A death is a happy event because we are going to continue with our lives; nothing stops. Death is a continuation of life. That person will live more peacefully now because he has fulfilled part of his destiny."

Majeobaje is greeted constantly by all who pass in front of us.

"The children of Yemayá are always giving presents," he tells me. "That is why people like us so much. People like to receive gifts."

"Well, Maje. May I call you Maje?"

"Of course; everyone does."

Maje goes on telling me about the two sides to life.

"Olofi wanted the world to contain everything. That is why he gave Oddudúa, the eldest, the task of creating the universe. Oddudúa had a great deal of experience because he had fought against other nations and emerged victorious. He founded a city and made it just as Olofi wanted it to be. Oddudúa is life and death, white and black. His children dress in these colors and sometimes wear parrot feathers on their heads, but the color white always predominates.

"Oddudúa decided that there should be rich and poor people in the world, the healthy and the sick, the good and the bad, blacks and albinos, and so it was. There is no need to feel bad when one sees a legless man in the market dragging himself along and begging.

"Oddudúa knew exactly what he was doing. He made some people blind or one-eyed and he even made humans without heads who die at birth and animals like the crab that walk backward. Thus the world is rich and varied. That is why there is a saying that a man should never weep; a man who weeps is just making a noise."

In Lagos, as in Cotonou, any vehicle may be a taxi: a motorbike, an old car, a Mercedes. I stop the first one that passes. I say good-bye to Maje using a Muslim greeting: "Ala Malekun."

"Malekun Ala,"[86] he answers with a conspiratorial smile, the smile of a wise man. An attachment to the land and an industrious nature typify the Yoruba. They are a people of vague origins, and their history is full of contradictory phases. Conquered, rebellious, capable of creating kingdoms and even empires, the

Yoruba are anchored to a firm mythological base and to a cosmogonic vision that is much richer and more profound than that
of other peoples in this region of Africa. Even the contingencies
of slavery could not damage this treasure of the imagination. In
an uninhibited fashion, they talk about slavery in a very self-con-
fident manner. They do not appear to bear a grudge. On the contrary, they tell anecdotes about resistance to oppression, and they
feel proud of their ancestors. Abdeola tells how his forebears
returned to Nigeria because they gained their freedom through
their own efforts. The story sounds odd, vague.

Abdeola is Yoruba but Muslim. He wears white and a cap with
gold threads. He carries an *iroke*, a flywhisk made from elephant
hair with an ivory handle. He is a highly respected tribal chief
and a historian of his people. We speak of the sacrifices and the
deeds of the Lucumís in Cuba. I tell him of the huge numbers of
slaves who hanged themselves from guásima trees because they
longed to return to their native land. I tell him that many tied ker-
chiefs around their necks or put on bracelets and anklets so that
when they reached Nigeria they could be identified by their relatives. These tokens were a sign of rebellion and carried the greet-
ings of their kinsmen in Cuba.

Over two million Africans arrived on the island during the
period of the slave trade. The majority belonged to the Bantu or
Kwa language families. The Yoruba belong to the latter. This figure amazes Abdeola, who, although he is Muslim, knows more
about the culture of this people than most and also how to interpret the Ifa oracle. His forefathers came from Oyo, the kingdom
of Changó, the fourth king of that land and a chief of the Ogboni
society,[87] so the historian tells me. I tell him that Ifa has been preserved and enriched in Cuba. The most complex African divination system is widespread throughout Cuba. There are thousands
of babalaos, its officiants, there. Orula—that is, Ifa—rules the
life of many Cubans.

"The babalaos are the owners of the secrets," Abdeola tells me.

"But you do not consult the divining tray," I reply. "You are Muslim."

He gives me an ironic look. I do not expect an answer. I recall the confession made by the minister of culture in Cotonou. "No one can do without Ifa, neither the Christians nor the practitioners of other religions. Ifa is in everything because it is not a religion; it is a divination system."

Thus I understand many things. I understand Abdeola and the Yoruba, Ibo, Fon and Mina people. Ifa rules the lives of people in a large part of southwestern Nigeria and of many others farther afield.

"They go to church during the day, but when they are in trouble they consult the divining tray, they turn to Ifa," Abdeola confirms.

The origin of Ifa is also nebulous. No one knows for certain where it came from. Some say that its birthplace was the town of Ketu in northern Benin, others that it was Oyo. But no one really knows its place of origin. However, of all the cults of the Yoruba people, the most popular, the most frequently visited, is Ifa. Neither the Hausa influence of the Muslim north nor Christianity and its offshoots have been able to destroy this secret divination cult, which is much more complex than the tarot or the I Ching.

For Abdeola, Ifa originated in Oyo, and there he was able to develop his gifts as a diviner and healer. This is the basis of the myths and legends, though naturally, each gives a different version.

Abdeola presents me with a small clay pipe, a baton and a necklace of leather and little bronze disks. For him, this getup forms part of tradition. Tradition is represented in Nigeria. It is something sacrosanct. Even when one does not belong to the old religion of the orishas, they are there, in the stones, in rivers, in the branches and foliage of trees like Iroko. One speaks to them, one chides them, one demands things from them because most of them used to be mortals. They are not intangible beings but corporeal. They are not to be found at the top of an altar, or in the direction of any Mecca, but in contact with the earth. The strength of these cults lies here, in that direct dialogue, in that almost carnal relationship.

While Abdeola proudly tells me the history of his compatriots, chapters from the work of Wole Soyinka come into my head: Aké, the world of the *egungun*,[88] the world of Changó, king of Oyo, of the warrior god Oggún, of Obbatalá Alláguna. Abdeola, teacher of history and Muslim journalist, is still unaware that these gods are found in Cuba. One would have to introduce him to the tangled forest—*ewefinda*[89]—of Lydia Cabrera and to the work of Fernando Ortiz. But that would have to wait. The Ifa divining tray will determine our next meeting.

Sitting at my writing desk I now contemplate my house in Havana, my house with its long corridors and open doors. Olorun, the sun, beats down on me as I write these lines. Alongside old pieces inherited from my family and works by painters of my generation, the Yoruba masks from Ife, the carved seat from Marina market, Elegguá in the doorway with a jacket of white thorns and a staff with the face of Oddudúa, founder of the Yoruba nation—a gift from Abdeola.

The ancient gods preserved this culture from the winds and tides. The slave ship and the barracoon served as the catalysts of a patrimony that is now a symbol of our life.

In my memory, my journey to the land of the orishas appears like a beautiful strip of light. In my memory too, since my return from Africa, Paris, the most beautiful city in the world, seems to me rather like an overstocked luxurious grocer's shop.

NOTES

1. The name given to Africans of Bantu origin in Cuba. (Unless otherwise indicated, all footnotes are the translator's.)

2. Fernando Ortiz, acknowledged as the pioneer of the study of Afro-Cuban culture, developed the theory of *transculturación*, as a critique of Herskovits' theory of acculturation, which he felt assumed that a superior culture would induce the transformation of supposedly inferior cultures. Transculturation, on the other hand, referred to the process whereby two cultures—in the case of Cuba, the Hispanic and the African—mutually influence each other to create something new.

3. The Abakuá secret society has its origin in the Ekpe secret society of the Cross River region of what is today Nigeria. Arará is the name by which groups of Adja-Fon origin became known in Cuba. The Yoruba, known as Lucumí in Cuba, are from the southwestern region of Nigeria.

4. *Pwatakí* or *patakí*, myths of the orishas (see n. 7 below).

5. "My son."

6. Lubbeo, title given to Changó that refers to his kingship.

7. *Orishas* are deified ancestors who established control over natural forces. They act as intermediaries between mankind and the Supreme Deity. Because of the influence of Catholicism, orishas are sometimes also referred to as *santos* (saints).

8. *Olofi*, "Sovereign Ruler." The influence of Catholicism in Cuba has resulted in the various names for the Yoruba supreme god being equated with the members of the Holy Trinity.

9. *Olodumare*, "Almighty One."

10. *Olorun*, "Owner or Lord of Heaven."

11. São Paolo, Brazil: Círculo Do Livro, 1975.

12. *Ebora*, "deity."

13. *Olúo*, high-ranking Ifá diviner who is also a babalocha.

14. *Babalawo*, literally "father of the secrets"; an Ifá diviner.

15. *Opele, okuele,* or *okpele,* chain used for divination. It consists of eight seed pods or pieces of metal attached to the chain at regular intervals, each of which has a convex and a concave side. The figure is divined from the number of convex or convex sides that appear when the chain

is thrown on the ground. The babalawo uses either a divining chain or sixteen palm nuts to produce the figure that is called an *odu* or *oddún*.

16. Diloggún divination is also known as sixteen-cowry divination, as the shells are thrown to produce a figure that is then interpreted for the client. Ifa divination is more prestigious, but is less common in the diaspora than diloggún.

17. *Babalocha*, m., *iyalocha*, f.; an orisha priest(ess) who has initiated others.

18. *Canto de puya*, song in which insults are hurled at an orisha to express dissatisfaction.

19. Sound is produced by stroking the grooves in the gourd with a stick.

20. *Moyubar*, to salute the ritual ancestors. This is done at the beginning of every ceremony.

21. Miguel Barnet, *Biography of a Runaway Slave* (Willimantic, Conn.: Curbstone Press, 1994), p. 17.

22. *Ilé ocha* or *ilé orisha*, literally "house of the orisha," temple house, normally the home of an iyalocha or babalocha.

23. *Palo mambó*, stick used for performing exorcisms.

24. *Acheré*, rattle used to call the god.

25. Regla, a town situated across the bay from Havana.

26. Ritual in honor of a deity, accompanied by drumming and dancing and possession trance.

27. *Iruke*, fly whisk made from the tail of a horse.

28. *Babalú ayé*, literally "father of the world." Term of address for Sopona, the Yoruba god of smallpox.

29. *Escoba amarga* (*Parthenium hysterophorus*), a plant much used in Cuban folk medicine.

30. *Libreta (de santero)*, collection of rituals and prayers written down in a book for a santero's personal use.

31. Nonnatus (Not Born), Catalan saint whose name derives from the fact that he was taken from his mother's womb after her death in labor.

32. *Moddú pue*, "Thank you."

33. *Cabildo (de nación)*, mutual aid association in colonial Cuba for Africans, both slave and free.

34. These were Cuban versions of African masquerades. They were popular in processions to celebrate feast days of the Catholic calendar and during Carnival.

35. Volunteer in the pro-Spanish militia of the Ten Years' War against Spain (1868–78).

36. Member of the Abakúa secret society, an all-male brotherhood that has

its origins in the Cross River area of southeastern Nigeria. It always experienced more repression by the authorities than the Afro-Cuban religious cult groups. This was partly because members were required to be brave and defiant and fights sometimes broke out between rival *potencias* (lodges).

37. *Taita, tata*, term used to address a practitioner of the Congo religions, e.g., Taita Andrés, literally "papa."

38. *Capataz*, head of the cabildo, literally "overseer, foreman."

39. Lydia Cabrera, *Reglas de congo, palo monte, mayombe* (Miami, Fla.: Peninsular Printing Inc., 1979), pp. 15–16. Lydia Cabrera was Ortiz's sister-in-law, but her own interest in Afro-Cuban forms emerged during her studies into Oriental art in Paris in the late 1920s.

40. *Tata nganga*, priest of palo monte who possesses a nganga and usually heads a temple house.

41. *Regla*, the term used for the differing Afro-Cuban religious practices *Regla de Ocha* and *Reglas Congas*, derives from the *reglamentos*, the rules of the *cabildos de nación*.

42. Miguel Barnet, *Biography of a Runaway Slave*, pp. 33–34.

43. Cabrera, op. cit., p. 213.

44. *Tierra*, literally "land."

45. Female position in a cabildo equivalent to that of *capataz*.

46. Cabrera, op. cit., pp. 60–61.

47. *Palos del monte*, literally "sticks" or "trees from the forest."

48. The terminology recalls the anti-Semitism of the Iberian Roman Catholic Church; *judío* is "bad," and *cristiano* is "good."

49. Barnet, op. cit., pp. 123–24.

50. *Ndoki*, "sorcerer" in KiKongo.

51. Nsambi, Sambia Mpungu, supreme deity of the BaKongo and related cultures.

52. Walterio Carbonell, *Mayombe en Cuba* (Havana, 1967).

53. *Prenda*, literally "pawn" or "treasure." In Cuban palo monte, a power object, the equivalent of the BaKongo nkisi.

54. *Solar*, tenement house.

55. Cabrera, op. cit., p. 93.

56. *Gangarria*, brass instrument.

57. *Alcahuete*, literally "pimp."

58. "Makuta Cockerel."

59. Cabrera, op. cit., pp. 77–78.

60. *Tumbadora*, large conga drum.

61. *Guateca*, small hoe.
62. Argeliers León, *Artes plásticas* (Havana: Dirección General de Cultura, Ministerio de Educación, No. 1, 1960), p. 28.
63. *Garabato*, long forked pole.
64. *Palenque*, settlement of runaway slaves.
65. *Firma*, magic sign, signature, cosmogram.
66. *Perro de prenda*, literally "dog of a prenda," term used to describe someone who is possessed.
67. Leovigildo López, "Las firmas de los santos," in *Actas del Folklore* (Havana) 1, no. 5 (1961).
68. Cabrera, op. cit., p. 126.
69. Barnet, op. cit., pp. 119–20.
70. Cabrera, op. cit., p. 124.
71. *Anima Sola*, Lonely Soul.
72. *Omó orisha*, child of an orisha, i.e., an initiate.
73. *Agó*, "Hello"; "Go well."
74. *Moforibale*, "I salute you."
75. *Cascarilla* or *efun*, white substance made from eggshells and used for ritual purposes.
76. Mina.
77. Don Francisco "Cha Cha" de Souza (1754–1849) was an important figure in the trans-Atlantic slave trade based in the port of Ouidah.
78. *Marímbula*, xylophonelike instrument.
79. *Loa* or *Iwa*, the name used in the diaspora to denote the spirits which are known as vodun in Africa.
80. *Comparsa*, group participating in Cuban carnival processions.
81. *Escudo real*, an old Brazilian coin, used ironically to refer to the gold-colored Cuban peso coin.
82. *Aché*, sacred power.
83. *Ajiaco*, Cuban stew.
84. *Ború boyé*, expression used for greeting babalawos.
85. *Iba e tonú tonú*, expression used for greeting the ancestors.
86. *Salaam aleykum*, peace be with you.
87. Ogboni, secret society responsible for maintaining social and political order.
88. *Egungun*, masquerades representing the ancestors.
89. *Ewefinda*, sacred plants and herbs used in Afro-religious practice.

ACKNOWLEDGEMENTS

The translator would like to thank Miguel Barnet for his kindness and willingness to help with translation and other queries, and Mayra Morán, Josephine Henrietta Pryce, and the rest of the staff of the Fundación Fernando Ortiz in Havana. Many thanks to Enrique de Cepeda Grillo and Miguel Ángel Bataille Soto for their expert and invaluable help with translation, to Guillermo Fernández Moret for answering questions on religious matters, and to Vicente Fabá Calderón for assistance with all of the above as well as support and encouragement during my stay in Cuba. Many thanks also to Adriana Dieguez of the Agencia Literaria Latinoamericana.

The publisher would like to thank the following for providing photos and maps and permission to use them in this book.

Miguel Barnet: map, illustrations and photos pp. 12, 13, 20, 25, 31, 39, 45, 51, 53, 56, 61, 64, 68, 80, 85, 87, 92, 96, 108, 116, 120, 130, 132

Jesús Guanche: illustrations pp. 1, 36, 42, 79, 99, 103, 106, 111

Holger Pöhlmann and Anthrovision, Munich, Germany:
© Holger Pöhlmann. Photos pp. i, 6, 10, 29, 59, 71, 94
© Marco Casanova cover and pp. 4, 34, 76, 114, 123, 127
© Reinhard Oefele p. 23
© Valdonio Berrío pp. 27, 49

Robin Law: © Robin Law map on p. 16

Markus Wiener Publishers Archives: 3, 15, 17, 72, 73, 77, 101, 113, 125, 135

From: Leo Frobenius, Kulturgeschichte Afrikas, Zurich: Phaidon Verlag, 1933: 137, 142

Thanks to Curbstone Press for permission to quote excerpts from Miguel Barnet's *Biography of a runaway slave* (English trans. W. Nick Hill).

David Lanter, Michael Figueroa, Benjamin Arnel Tilentino, Stephen Kirin, Marina Carmen Smith, Lupe Herrera, and Steve Sanderson of the Digital Computer Cartographic Laboratory of UCSB: map on p. 72, from Robert O. Collins, ed., *Problems in African History,* vol. 1, *The Precolonial Centuries*, p. 96.